Sadly, the role of the Holy
often ignored or simply ass
thing He said and did was of the Spirit. And He promised that
when He left, His followers would have that same Spirit within.
Jeff Kennedy and this book will help you better understand the
person and work of the Holy Spirit. I recommend you read it!

—LARRY OSBORNE
Author, *Sticky Church* and *Sticky Teams*
Pastor, North Coast Church, Vista, CA

Many Christian efforts have left the world unimpressed and the
church disappointed. Jeff Kennedy points us to the neglect of the
Holy Spirit as the culprit. This book helps the reader make sure
that all our work is empowered and aligned with God and His
purpose. I like the practicality of Jeff's presentation; he makes it
easy to think and pray about the issues.

—BILL HULL
Author, *Choose the Life* and *Jesus Christ Disciple Maker*

Sometimes our neglect of a thing is benign—the garden we fail
to weed, the dog we don't walk. But other times our neglect is
tragic: the daughter we never tell is beautiful, the phone call we
need to make but don't. Jeff Kennedy puts his finger on a tragic
neglect: our vexing, perplexing tendency to reduce the Holy Spirit
to mere doctrine—indeed, to doctrinal hairs that we then split
finer and finer—and to never know Him as a person. Thankfully
Jeff makes up, with passion and intelligence, for this neglect, and
reintroduces us to the Other One, in all His glorious mysterious
fullness. Timely and timeless.

—MARK BUCHANAN
Associate Professor, Pastoral Theology, Ambrose University
Author, *Your Church Is Too Safe*

This readable and balanced book treats a wide range of aspects of the Spirit's work. It is inviting and will encourage readers in their relationship with God.

—CRAIG KEENER, PhD
Professor, New Testament, Asbury Theological Seminary
Author, *IVP Bible Background Commentary*

The Spirit scares even Christians, because when the Spirit fills us, something mighty can happen, and many of us prefer the ordinary. Jeff Kennedy's *Father, Son, and the Other One* will disturb you in a good way because it will open your eyes to the extraordinary life God wants for you. A welcome addition for renewal in our day.

—SCOT MCKNIGHT, PhD
Professor, New Testament, Northern Seminary
Author, *The King Jesus Gospel*

I am delighted to recommend Jeff Kennedy's *Father, Son, and the Other One* as a fine work on the role of the Holy Spirit in the life of the believer. Jeff thoughtfully navigates between theology and practical application, providing the reader with a balanced and highly engaging treatment of an often-neglected, but absolutely crucial, aspect of the Christian life. *Father, Son, and the Other One* will be a valuable resource for followers of Jesus who long for the kind of relationship with God that we hear so much about but seldom actually experience in our daily lives. I would like to see everyone in my church read this book.

—JOE HELLERMAN, PhD
Professor, NT Language and Literature,
Talbot School of Theology
Author, *When the Church Was a Family*
Copastor, Oceanside Christian Fellowship

It is rare to find a book that is inspiring, informative, insightful, and also fun to read. Jeff Kennedy has provided a gem to the body of Christ in *Father, Son, and the Other One*. This book will encourage and challenge you to fall in love again with the Holy Spirit. It will make you hungry and desperate for more of His presence in the church. Jeff's theology is solid and his case compelling. If you want to understand more of the Spirit, this extraordinary book is a must-read.

—KURT BUBNA
Author, *Epic Grace: Chronicles of a Recovering Idiot*
Lead Pastor, Eastpoint Church, Spokane, WA

With literary edginess, uncommon wit, and engaging parables Jeff Kennedy introduces us to not just "the other One" of a triune God but someone worthy of truly being our significant other—a Holy Spirit who is very much alive and well and waiting to flourish within us if only we get to know Him for who He really is.

—RONNA SNYDER
Author, *Hot Flashes From Heaven*

Jeff Kennedy has provided the evangelical community with a well-written, highly accessible, yet thoughtful introduction to what the Bible has to say about the Holy Spirit. I'm convinced that *Father, Son, and the Other One* can be effectively used by evangelical pastors to encourage church members toward a dynamic walk with Christ that is Spirit empowered as well as biblically informed. No little goal, this! Here's a book that represents a big step toward its realization!

—GARY TYRA, DMin
Professor, Biblical and Practical Theology,
VanGuard University
Author, *Christ's Empowering Presence*

Father, Son, and the Other One is the result of years of studious practice. As a pastor, I deeply appreciate Jeff's ability to balance orthodoxy with practice. One without the other can produce unfruitful outcomes. I highly recommend this book for followers of Christ everywhere!

—ROBERT J. RHODEN, DMIN
Pastor, Commonwealth Chapel, Richmond, VA

Jeff Kennedy enters the dialogue on the often-marginalized third person of the Trinity and leads us on an engaging journey of discovery—a journey that personalizes the role of the Holy Spirit in the life of every believer!

—KENT MANKINS, PhD
Lead Pastor, Valley Assembly, Spokane Valley, WA

Pastor Kennedy offers a balanced approach to the person of the Holy Spirit. I appreciate his thoroughly biblical approach as well as his clear, personal, relevant writing style. This book will be appreciated by biblical scholars, church leaders, and all earnest Christians who perhaps need to be reintroduced to the Holy Spirit. This book encourages me, a pastor, that the Holy Spirit is not simply "the help," but that He is the God who has invaded our lives with transforming presence.

—STEVE LAYNE
Pastor, Life Church, Upper Marlboro, MD
President, Clinton Christian School
Associate Professor, New Testament Greek
and Biblical Studies

FATHER, SON,

AND

THE

OTHER ONE

JEFF KENNEDY

THE ART OF AUTHENTIC FAITH

Most CHARISMA HOUSE BOOK GROUP products are available at special quantity discounts for bulk purchase for sales promotions, premiums, fund-raising, and educational needs. For details, write Charisma House Book Group, 600 Rinehart Road, Lake Mary, Florida 32746, or telephone (407) 333-0600.

FATHER, SON, AND THE OTHER ONE by Jeff Kennedy
Published by Passio
Charisma Media/Charisma House Book Group
600 Rinehart Road
Lake Mary, Florida 32746
www.charismahouse.com

Unless otherwise noted, all Scripture quotations are from the Holy Bible, New International Version. Copyright © 1973, 1978, 1984, International Bible Society. Used by permission.

Scripture quotations marked ESV are from the Holy Bible, English Standard Version. Copyright © 2001 by Crossway Bibles, a division of Good News Publishers. Used by permission.

Scripture quotations marked NAS are from the New American Standard Bible, copyright © 1960, 1962, 1963, 1968, 1971, 1972, 1973, 1975, 1977, 1995 by The Lockman Foundation. Used by permission. (www.Lockman.org)

Scripture quotations marked NET are from the New English Translation, copyright © 1996-2006 by Biblical Studies Press, LLC. http://netbible.com. All rights reserved. This material is available in its entirety as a free download or online use at http://netbible.org/.

Scripture quotations marked NKJV are from the New King James Version of the Bible. Copyright © 1979, 1980, 1982 by Thomas Nelson, Inc., publishers. Used by permission.

Cover design by Lisa Rae Cox
Design Director: Bill Johnson

Visit the author's websites at jeffkennedy.tv and eastpointchurch.org/ministries/discipleship-training/; also connect with him at facebook.com/jeffscottkennedy and twitter.com/jeffscottk.

Library of Congress Control Number: 2013951548
International Standard Book Number: 978-1-62136-510-5
E-book ISBN: 978-1-62136-511-2

While the author has made every effort to provide accurate telephone numbers and Internet addresses at the time of publication, neither the publisher nor the author assumes any responsibility for errors or for changes that occur after publication.

First edition

14 15 16 17 18 — 9 8 7 6 5 4 3 2 1
Printed in the United States of America

To Kerri—my beloved accomplice in life. You are my friend, my partner, my love. Your kindness and gentleness of heart have made it possible for me to experience God's presence in a most profound and unexpected way.

To the children—Tyler, Hayden, Logan, and Karlee. I wrote this book for you, my little darlings. Someday when you're old enough, Daddy's explanations won't require explanations. Until then, enjoy the stories.

To Mom—your passion for God's presence was a most effective apologetic. You taught me that the best evidence for God is God Himself. Thank you.

To Skip—I know you prefer to be called "Stan" as you fly all over the country leading high-powered business meetings. But to me you'll always be Skip, the homemade nunchuck-wielding, ramp-jumping, neighborhood daredevil.

But most of all, this book is dedicated to the Father, the Son, and the Holy Spirit. The flame You've lit in me will burn forever. May every word and every sentence of this book bring honor and glory to You.

Contents

PART THREE:
Embrace the Mystery
How do I embrace life in the Spirit today?

Acknowledgments

A BIG THANK-YOU TO:

- Steve Ziemke, for helping me fish my books out of the bushes at Tucker High. I wouldn't be here doing what I'm doing without your leadership and guidance.

- Dr. H. Robert Rhoden, for teaching me how to preach the Word. When I was sitting in your church as a teenager, your fiery teaching seemed touched by heaven itself.

- The late Dr. Daniel Pecota, for talking me into taking Greek. You never lived to see your prophecy to me come true. Can't wait someday to give you a good report when I see you again on the shores of heaven.

- A special thanks to my pastor, life-mentor, and friend Kurt Bubna, for showing me that real men cry and real pastors passionately love God above all else. You are the real deal, my friend. Someday when I grow up, I'm going to be just like you.

- My doctoral mentor at Talbot, Michael Wilkins, PhD, for showing me what it means to be a humble scholar of the Word. The last four years sitting under your teaching has been one of the greatest experiences of my life. I hope you like the dissertation.

- The radical, hilarious, and superhumanly gifted pastors at Eastpoint Church: Kurt, Brian, Matt, and Nathan. For I am not ashamed of my "bro-mance" with each of you, for it is the power of wit unto uproarious laughter. I cannot imagine doing ministry without you. I hope we can work together until Jesus comes back.

- The congregation at Eastpoint Church. Serving you is one of the greatest privileges and joys of my life.

- The team at Charisma House and the Passio imprint: From my first phone conversation with Jevon, I could tell we were going to hit it off. Thanks to Jason, Woodley, Ann, Jevon, and the entire team there. Thanks for your patience and believing in this project.

- Thanks to my literary agent, Kimberly Shumate, for all your hard work. Your knowledge and experience have been indispensible in this process. Thank you for being accessible and very engaged. I'm so blessed to be represented by you.

Introduction
BEEN THERE, DONE THAT, BOUGHT THE T-SHIRT

I HAD ALWAYS WANTED to see Mount Rushmore. To tell the truth, I had no idea where the national monument was even located. The only reason why I had an opportunity to see it was because my wife and I were moving from Minnesota back to the Pacific Northwest. We found out that the famous monument was just outside of Rapid City, South Dakota, and we decided it would be a worthwhile excursion. So after a long and frenetic day of running errands and packing our moving van, we set out to experience this man-made wonder.

However, the long and numbing drive through South Dakota to get to the monument is what I would call a "non-experience." We saw the occasional bent tree and abandoned shack tilted in the direction of South Dakota's unrelenting wind. We endured five hundred miles of billboard advertisements for "Wall Drug" and refueled at the occasional gas station where live bait could be purchased from coin-operated vending machines (who knew?). By the time we reached the other side of the state, our anticipation had been long nourished by hours of seeing nothing in all directions. We eventually made it to the other side of the state and got a great view of the barren spires of South Dakota's Badlands.

We were so glad to finally arrive in Rapid City, and we began our ascent up the mountain to the hallowed site. The engine of my rental van strained and sputtered all the way, and we barely made it to the top. We parked the van and walked toward the entrance on wobbly legs. We were groggy and eager and ready to be blown away. Unfortunately, a thick mist from the Badlands hid the sculptures. Disappointment set in as we realized that we were going to miss seeing the renowned Rushmore faces.

So we did the next best thing.

We ducked into the information center, meandered through the museum, and absorbed all of the interesting facts on the history of Mount Rushmore. We poured over brochures, looked at old photographs, and bought some items from the gift shop. If we couldn't see the famous sculptures, we figured we might as well buy a postcard and a T-shirt to prove that we were there.

After about an hour, the clouds unexpectedly receded, and my wife and I emerged from the information center for a firsthand encounter with the towering monument. We stepped up to the edge of the viewing area, and there they were—forever enshrined in stone: Washington, Jefferson, Lincoln, and Roosevelt. We stood there for thirty minutes, warming in the sun and marveling at that feat of engineering. We would never read our brochures or see photos of the monument the same again.

I wonder how many Christian lives resemble the first part of that story. We may have strolled through the museums of church history, listened to some audio lectures on theology, and read all of the right doctrinal brochures. We have believed everything we were told to believe. And we know we have a mysterious connection at some level with the Holy Spirit, but regrettably it is too mysterious. We ache for more. And we suspect it's not too far out of reach. We are tired of only learning about God and want the clouds to part—we want to encounter Him for ourselves as we step into the full beam of His glorious presence.

What You'll Find

I wrote *Father, Son, and the Other One* for every believer who has ever wondered if the Christian faith is more than mere creeds and doctrines and denominational distinctives. It's for all of those who need reassurance that the Jesus of history still dwells in us by the Spirit of God. It's for every believer who longs to tap into God's presence as a transforming, empowering reality.

Part 1 of the book will identify the problem: the Spirit has largely been marginalized in American Christianity. This can happen as we replace the work of the Spirit and faith with well-intentioned but Spirit-less innovation. Or it can happen as we overemphasize supernatural manifestations, neglecting the Spirit as a person who desires to be known in His own right. Beyond the bells and whistles of our gadget-driven worship services and spiritual manifestations, the Spirit is a person who wants to walk closely with us through life.

Part 2 will specifically address what the Spirit is doing in the world and the church today. We may be surprised to discover just how intimately He is at work in our lives as disciples. The Spirit does more than the discreet work of inner transformation. Though His first job is to transform us into the likeness of Jesus, all too often we have kept Him in the shadows busy with the invisible. We'll see that life in the Spirit should be characterized by both inner transformation and the attending phenomena—the manifestations of the Spirit.

A manifestation is a visible expression or a display of the Spirit's power. The Spirit is manifest in our character transformation as we produce fruit for the kingdom. And the Spirit outfits us for life in the kingdom through spiritual gifts. It is this aspect of the Spirit's work that can sometimes make us uncomfortable. In the chapters that follow, we'll find that the coming of the Spirit signaled to the apostles that God's supernatural kingdom rule had broken into their fallen world. We live between the times—between this age and the already-but-not-yet age of God's kingdom.

Part 3 will outline how you can embrace the awesome and unwieldy mystery of God's presence. We must embrace the Spirit by faith. And this is sometimes risky business that will shred the safe nests we've feathered within the church. A comfort zone, by definition, is an anxiety-neutral space where we are never challenged and where we avoid anything that may be "unsafe." But God never intended the Christian life to be anxiety-neutral. We need all of the resources of heaven to meet the challenges of "the valley of the shadow of death" (Ps. 23:4).

After all, that's where we spend most of our time.

That's where we live.

By contrast, verdant pastures and quiet waters are a soldier's respite, a warrior's refuge—not a resort for complacent and fightless sheep. Jesus said, "In the world you will have tribulation. But take heart; I have overcome the world" (John 16:33, ESV). In this world we are battered by trials, stalked by the enemy, and ridiculed by society. This world means to siphon the life from us bit by bit. But Jesus has promised to send us One who will outfit us for kingdom life. This is why we so desperately need an emphasis on the Spirit's work today—why we need to experience God in fresh and unexpected ways.

THE HIDDEN JESUS

Have you ever wondered why, when Jesus ascended into heaven, "a cloud hid him from their sight" (Acts 1:9)? There is something about the hiddenness of Jesus that is fascinating and disturbing in that passage. I can imagine the disciples with a similar look on their faces that my wife and I had at the Rushmore National Monument—expectant, wistful, longing. They were longing for Jesus to establish His kingdom on earth. They were anxious to take their places as His emissaries and the ambassadors of that new kingdom rule. But the kingdom wouldn't come as they had expected. The last question on their minds was, "Are you at this time going to restore the kingdom to Israel?" (v. 6). Jesus's answer, ostensibly, was, "No. That's not the plan." But they wouldn't have to wait very long. The kingdom age would materialize with the coming of the Spirit in ways that they could not possibly have anticipated.

Shortly after that, all believers were filled with the Spirit and began proclaiming the wonders of God. The coming of the Spirit is a fulfillment of the promise of new covenant made through Ezekiel (Ezek. 36:26) and Jeremiah (Jer. 31:31). Disciples are reborn, inwardly renewed, and empowered for life-witness. Jesus promised the disciples that He would send them "another Advocate" and that is exactly what He did at Pentecost (John 14:16, NLT).

Yet, the presence of the Spirit also guarantees us that a day is coming when the clouds that hid Jesus will part, the light of God's glory will shine, and the Son of God will reveal Himself. On that day our best sculptures and accomplishments in engineering won't hold a candle to Jesus's glorious face. On that day we will know as we are fully known, and what we are will be revealed in the moment of His return. So my prayer for you, dear disciple, is that from this day to that, you will recognize the One who walks with you through the badlands of life—the God of all comfort, the other Advocate—the Spirit.

PART ONE
BEYOND THE BELLS AND WHISTLES
Who is the Spirit, and why should we care?

THINK OF THE best gift you've ever received and hold the image of it in your mind. Got it? Good. Now try to remember why the gift was so special. It could have been something personal, like a homemade card, or something timely, like a check to help you pay your light bill. In the same way, Jesus promised to send believers the gift of the Holy Spirit. The gift of the Spirit was both personal and timely.

Part 1 of this book will identify that the Spirit has largely been marginalized in the Western branch of Christianity. This can happen as we minimize or even replace the Spirit with inventive and ingenious methods, or it can happen as we overdo it with regard to supernatural phenomena, neglecting the Spirit as a person who desires to be known in His own right. In Part 1 we'll examine why our culture perceives the church to be powerless and disconnected from daily realities. Beyond the bells and whistles of Spirit gifts and manifestations, we must begin to see the Spirit as the personal, transforming presence of God.

1

THE OTHER ONE

We've ignored the Spirit.

> The Holy Spirit, like the Father and the Son, is
> not just a doctrine, an idea, or an experience to be
> tagged on to the other doctrines and experiences
> of our Christian life. He is the God who has
> invaded our lives with his transforming presence.[1]
> —CRAIG KEENER—
> *Gift and Giver*

I FELT AS IF I just didn't matter.

I was the pastor of a brand-new church that met in the elementary school of a small town. The school was located right next door to the largest and fastest-growing church in our region. Each Sunday I would set up our sandwich-board sign by the road as droves of cars passed by on their way to the church next door.

"No worries," I told myself. "There are plenty of lost sheep to go around."

Not long after I started that small church, I decided to venture out into the neighborhood to meet some people. My last stop was the home of an elderly couple. I introduced myself as the pastor of a new church in town and was welcomed into their home with enthusiasm. After a long day of hearing "Get lost. We're not interested!", I was glad to finally make a connection with someone. The elderly lady announced down the hallway that the "pastor" was there to visit. Her husband bounded out of the back room and seemed eager to meet me. He vigorously shook my hand and offered me a comfortable chair.

Unfortunately they had mistaken me for the pastor of the megachurch next door to mine. Calling me by his name, they remarked what a privilege it was to have me (or him) in their home and how much they loved my (or his) preaching. They went on and on about me (or him).

Beads of sweat rolled down my forehead.

When I finally got a word in, I broke it to them. "Um. Well, that's all great. But *ahem*, actually, I'm the pastor of the church next door to that one. We're new in town, and so I wanted to—" The elderly woman interrupted me. Her smile morphed into a frown. Her glow diminished beneath the haze of disappointment.

"Oh. I see. You're the pastor of that *other one*."

And so I was.

We chatted politely, and I put on my best poker face, trying to conceal how awkward I felt in that moment. But nothing could hide it. I shuffled out of the door mumbling a rehearsed prayer, thanking God for the opportunity to grow through humility or something lame like that. I slid into my car seat, politely waved, and drove away in embarrassment. Though it was probably just the fatigue of a long and fruitless day, I left that house feeling like the *other* pastor—as if I didn't matter. Not one bit.

Have you ever been there? Many résumés sent but few return calls. You were qualified for that promotion but passed up in favor of a less experienced coworker. Or maybe you're in a marriage where you are essentially treated like a nonentity.

Many of us know what it's like to be picked last, overlooked, or politely dismissed.

THIRD PERSON OR THIRD WHEEL?

It may shock you to discover that God also knows how it feels to be overlooked and ignored. The story above is an analogy of how I believe many Christians relate to the Holy Spirit—the third person of the Trinity. Sure, we pray to our Father in heaven and close in Jesus's name. We may even baptize people in the name of the Father, the Son, and the Spirit. But it's that last person in our baptismal formula who usually gets left out of our day-to-day experience. The Spirit is largely ignored in America as a present transforming reality. I have often wondered how it must grieve God's Spirit to be treated with such indifference—as if He's just that *other* member of the Trinity who doesn't matter all that much.

Over the years I've observed that Christianity in the West tends to marginalize the Holy Spirit in one of three ways: disbelief, indifference, or sidelining. In chapters 1 and 2 we'll explore each of these in that order. In chapter 3 we'll also explore how easy it is to ignore the Spirit while fixating on miraculous phenomena.

A Dove on a Stained-Glass Window

"I don't believe in all that Spirit mumbo-jumbo!" my friend Kevin told me. We were having an intense conversation over whether the Holy Spirit was real or not.

"Just seems like a bunch of nonsense," he groused, rolling his eyes and folding his arms.

Now, Kevin wasn't a hardened atheist or a confused agnostic. He was a self-identified believer in Jesus who went to church with his family on occasion. He had no problem relating to God as a heavenly Father or believing that Jesus died for his sins. But the notion that God is presently at work in us by the person of the Holy Spirit sounded like religious jargon to him.

We may be tempted to chalk this up as an extreme case. Regrettably this example is the rule, not the exception. The Barna Group, a research organization in Ventura, California, found that only 25 percent of American Christians believe in the *existence* of the Holy Spirit.[2] Barna also found that younger generations were less likely to believe in and engage with the Spirit.[3] This statistic is alarming when one considers the mass exodus from church life among eighteen- to thirty-four-year-olds in America.

This means that, for most professing Christians, the Holy Spirit is nothing more than a symbol of the faith—a dove on a stained-glass window. This "Spirit-less" version of Christianity is dangerous for several reasons.

First, it compromises biblical truth. Jesus told Nicodemus that unless he was born again by the Spirit, he would never enter God's kingdom (John 3:3, 5–8). The church was born on the Day of Pentecost, when the Spirit of God baptized and filled every believer (Acts 2:2). The Christian faith is a lot of things, but it is *nothing* without the Spirit. We may engrave His name in the bedrock of our historic creeds, but without His presence we are not of Christ at all.[4]

Second, Spirit-less Christianity jettisons our mandate. Christianity is not a nice family religion. It is a living, active, and missional enterprise. God did not send Jesus so that you and I could inherit a harmless delusion that makes us feel better when we're sad. If we make the mistake of treating the Spirit as nothing more than a theological abstraction, an amorphous concept, or a vague idea, we will utterly fail to disciple the nations and the next generation. This is why Jesus told the disciples to wait in Jerusalem for the Father's promise—God's empowering presence (Acts 1:4–8).[5] Take the Holy Spirit away from the church, and all we're left with is a grace-deficient, family-based cult.

How did we get here? I suggest that the widespread incredulity of the next generation is the result, or the fruit, of the previous generation's marginalization of the Spirit. We have ignored Him as a present reality in our midst even while insisting that parishioners learn rightly *about* Him. In effect, we have barred would-be worshippers from the fullness of the Spirit's experience while teaching them the Apostles' Creed.

LOOK BUT DON'T TOUCH

The first time I ever saw the Declaration of Independence I nearly got arrested. Housed in the Rotunda for the Charters of Freedom in Washington DC, the historic document is old and fragile and is encased behind some type of bulletproof glass.

When I got my chance, I stepped up to view the celebrated manuscript. Probably because I have seen too many adventure movies, I put both hands on the glass and began meticulously inspecting this national treasure—all the wrinkles and folds and faded ink—as if I were looking for a secret encoded message or something. But I had gotten too close, way too close for the comfort of the armed guard standing next to the stone pedestal.

"Hands off the glass, sir. You can look, just don't touch. OK?" The uniformed guard appeared to be as serious as a heart attack. And since I was not in the mood to be Tasered and wrestled to the ground, I slowly backed away.

Growing up attending a small church in rural Virginia, I encountered certain boundaries when it came to experiencing God. I was told I could read the Bible, pray quietly, and learn church doctrine in Sunday school. I could think about God, and I could observe how He has acted in history with the saints of old. All of this was great. But the one thing I could never, *ever* do in that religious system was actually to encounter the Spirit for myself. I could look. But I could never quite touch.

At least not in any conspicuous sort of way.

What I often did encounter was a religious system that seemed to worship God from a distance. It was a system where Bible study and church attendance were the sole competencies of spiritual formation. And if we got out of line or went too far in our experience of God, well, the religious police were right there to make sure we just "looked" but didn't "touch." The Spirit was treated as if He were a fragile old document that needed to be protected from the masses.

CANNONBALL!

I introduced a little chaos into this tight religious environment on the occasion of my baptism as a young boy. Our congregation met in an iconic redbrick building with a white steeple like the mast of a ship stretching skyward. Our baptistery was a fiberglass tank built into the front of the sanctuary behind the choir benches. Two doors flanked the stage leading to dressing rooms for baptism candidates.

The night I was to be baptized I had an awesome idea. Instead of reverently gliding down the steps in a blue baptism robe looking like a floating Smurf, I thought I'd jump in and try out the water. So I hopped off the top step and splashed down into the baptism tank. The look on the preacher's face was a mix of kindness and caution. I could tell he wasn't sure what I might do next. And I could hear the collective gasps of an uptight congregation.

"Um. Mr. Kennedy. Is there anything you'd like to say on this occasion of your baptism in Christ?" I wasn't sure what I was supposed to be testifying about. So I blurted out what was on my mind in that moment.

"Man, this water is really cold!"

The congregation erupted in laughter but quickly composed themselves. After the pastor baptized me, I came up out of the water feeling a genuine sense of joy in the Holy Spirit. "Whoo hoo!" I shouted. I couldn't articulate my belief system in all of its particulars. I just knew that God was there with me.

Then I negotiated my way to the bottom of the wooden stairs, where my father was waiting with his belt in hand. I had disrupted the solemnity of that service with splashing and laughter. I had fist-pumped my way to history's first post-baptism spanking.

The people in that church were raised to believe that the words *spontaneous* and *sacred* did not belong in the same sentence. And as the congregation sang "Shall We Gather at the River," Dad made sure that he and I saw eye-to-eye on the issue of joyless religion.

An Awesome and Unwieldy Mystery

Over the years the church in America has become adept at establishing the boundaries, setting the limits of experience. We can believe the right stuff so long as we rope it off and keep it behind the protective glass of our institutional conventions and denominational distinctives. And if we fly too close to the sacred flame, we could find ourselves getting body-checked by the heresy police.

There's certainly nothing wrong with orderly worship. This is both biblical and necessary so that our message will be intelligible. Our worship must be doctrinally sound (1 Tim. 1:3), motivated by love (1 Cor. 13:1–3), but it must also be energized by God's awesome and unwieldy presence (1 Cor. 14:1). The Spirit inspires our experience, and we give direction and order to it (1 Cor. 14:39).

We're OK with the Spirit so long as we can keep Him occupied with the discreet work of inner transformation. You know, the invisible stuff. Yet we struggle with the notion that He wants to baptize and submerge us in new life—a joyous life.

A life that makes us dance and laugh and splash around with hope.

A life that transforms our status from "exiles and foreigners" to "sons of the Most High God."

It is also a life that can inspire stunned silence as we sit in fear and wonder of an awesome heavenly Father.

Out of the World Beyond Them

A. W. Tozer once remarked that the Spirit was sent to the disciples, "out of the world beyond them, over the threshold of their beings into the sanctum, sanatorium…into the deep of their spirit. There he would live and teach them and lead them, making them holy and giving them power."[6] This image of God's presence "spilling over" the threshold of our beings is rich and beautiful.

Jesus said, "The Spirit gives life" (John 6:63). Jesus is the source of that life, and the Spirit is its substance. This is why the

New Testament often interchanges the phrases "Spirit of Christ" and "Holy Spirit." Jesus's resurrection power has come to us, and He lives in us by the person of the Spirit. That simple, profound statement of Jesus, "The Spirit gives life," was fulfilled after He resurrected from the tomb. The Spirit reanimated eleven dead men as He moved over the threshold of their beings into the deep parts of them. The Spirit also revives us today. Reenacting the scene from the garden, Jesus leans over clay and dust, He cups His hands 'round our nostrils, and He breathes the Spirit's life into our dead souls. This is not the sort of gift that inspires indifference and boredom in the Christian life.

More Dangerous Than Open Dissent

Yet much of our church experience seems indifferent to the Spirit's existence. And if I've learned anything about Jesus over the years, it's that He has zero tolerance for my indifference. Indifference numbs me to the things that shred the heart of God. Jesus experienced this among His own audience and seemed genuinely surprised at the unresponsive, sleepy crowds in His hometown.

> Then Jesus began to denounce the towns in which most of his miracles had been performed, because they did not repent. "Woe to you, Korazin! Woe to you, Bethsaida! For if the miracles that were performed in you had been performed in Tyre and Sidon, they would have repented long ago in sackcloth and ashes. But I tell you, it will be more bearable for Tyre and Sidon on the day of judgment than for you. And you, Capernaum, will you be lifted to the skies? No, you will go down to the depths. If the miracles that were performed in you had been performed in Sodom, it would have remained to this day. But I tell you that it will be more bearable for Sodom on the day of judgment than for you."
>
> —Matthew 11:20–24

In the Old Testament God reserved this "woe" language for the most egregious offenders. So why would Jesus apply such a thunderous denouncement to His own neighborhood?

It wasn't that they did something to offend Him. They did *exactly nothing*. The sin of inaction brought judgment. The absence of passion, repentance, and faith brought His strongest condemnation. William Barclay once noted that indifference "does not burn a religion to death; it freezes it to death. It does not behead it. It slowly suffocates the life out of it."[7] Slowly. Surely. Until all that is left is the corpse of something that once moved with spark and verve.

The residents of Chorazin, Bethsaida, and Capernaum could have rejected Jesus or they could have welcomed Him. But they did neither. They neither followed His teachings nor protested His cause. Your critics may hate you. But at least with an angry mob, you know where you stand.

The passage in Matthew shows us that indifference is a more insidious threat than open dissent. At least the outlaw is wide awake to his own rebellion. The ancient inhabitants of Tyre, Sidon, and Sodom could have been confronted and debated and shown the error of their faulty belief systems. They could have experienced the miracles of the Spirit and responded with faith and repentance. Yet Jesus's best fireworks could not awaken the snoozing Galileans in Chorazin, Bethsaida, and Capernaum. Jesus taught us that apathetic religion is dangerous.

Jesus wanted to give His hearers in Galilee a gift that they frankly could not have comprehended—to make them truly "Spiritual," or *of the Spirit*. I'm sure these folks were as Torah observant and as pious as the next Jew. They surely thought of themselves as "spiritual." But genuine spirituality is always genuine Spirituality. Jesus wanted to offer the Spirit's life to them first (Matt. 10:5–6), but they rejected it and remained unresponsive to His message and mission.

There was no shortage of religion in that region. And there is no shortage of religion in the church today. Religion promises a one-size-fits-all approach to God. But this prefab spirituality is at odds with the unique work that the Spirit wants to do in each of us.

THE SPIRIT PEOPLE

What if your pastor announced this Sunday that the board of elders had met and decided to change the name of your church to "The Spirit People"? Would that freak you out? How do you think your neighborhood or community would respond to that name on your church sign?

Dr. Gordon Fee's massive tome on the Spirit entitled *God's Empowering Presence* established that when Paul used the Greek term *pneumatikos* (spiritual), he never used it to simply designate a person who was inwardly godly or religious, the way we mostly use it today.[8] When Paul used the term *pneumatikos* (spiritual), it was always to describe the believer's "Spirit life." That is, the disciple's defining orientation is a life that is energized by and pertains to the Spirit of God.[9] The Spirit always points us to Jesus. But then Jesus always fills us with the Spirit. So Spirit people are known as "Spiritual," not merely by the amorphous designation of "spiritual."

Paul goes so far as to call the Corinthian and Galatian Christians *pneumatikoi*—or "Spirit people." (See 1 Corinthians 2:6–3:1; 12:1–14:40; 15:44–46; Galatians 6:1.) These are two different churches that went off track but for different reasons. The Galatians began with powerful demonstrations of God in their midst but were in danger of abandoning the work of the Spirit for the works of Torah (the Law). Paul insisted that the Spirit people among them should gently restore that congregation to a life of genuine Spirit formation (Gal. 6:1).

In another case, the Corinthians overemphasized the manifestations of the Spirit and had undervalued character formation. Yet Paul regarded them as *pneumatikoi* (Spirit people) because it was the experienced reality of the Holy Spirit that set them apart from the pagan behavior and Greek philosophy into which they were dangerously drifting (1 Cor. 1:18–30).

In his letters to the Corinthians, Romans, Galatians, Ephesians, and Colossians, twenty-six different times Paul referred to their "Spirit life," and several times he suggested that these first-century believers were the "Spirit people."[10] I'd venture to guess that if there were a church today with the name "Spirit people" on its sign, it would be labeled weird and cultic. Don't worry. I'm sure this name change isn't on the agenda for your church's next board meeting.

There is no such thing as Christian spirituality. There is only Christian Spirituality. We cannot hope to achieve spiritual transformation by simply trying harder or believing all the right stuff or meditating for long hours in isolation, all of which are helpful. But we also need a genuine encounter with the living presence of God. All true believers have the Spirit. And all believers need to encounter Him in His fullness. What we badly need in our time are those who would respond in faith to Jesus and so become "the Spirit people."

A SOBERING REALITY

Given this emphasis on Spirit life in the New Testament, it is hard to imagine that only 25 percent of Christians today hold a firm belief in the person of the Holy Spirit. If that statistic is true, or anywhere near true, then we are facing an epic crisis in the church today. I believe it will become increasingly more difficult to pass our faith on to successive generations in America. Christianity cannot be seen as a credible option in a culture where it is reduced to a mere historic curiosity, devoid of wind and fire—absent the Spirit of life.

Our God is a tri-unity. He is one God who exists in three separate persons.

God the Father, from whom all blessings flow.

God the Son, who gave Himself for our sins.

And God the Spirit. The God who has "invaded our lives with transforming presence." Let's not dismiss Him. Let's not politely endure a doctrine class about Him while we move on to bigger and better strategies. And let's not settle for any version of the Christian faith that treats the Spirit as if He doesn't matter—as if He is just that *other* member of the Trinity. Let's become the Spirit people whom God intended for us to be.

In the next few chapters we'll discover what it means to be the Spirit people and how the modern church tends to either look like the Galatians or the Corinthians in their approach to Spirit life. Then we'll focus on how to reengage the life of the Spirit in our own time.

2

THERE'S NO APP FOR THAT

We've replaced the Spirit.

I often wonder if religion is the enemy of
God. It's almost like religion is what happens
when the Spirit has left the building.[1]
—BONO—
front man for U2

WE LIVE IN an age of spectacular innovation. It's hard to
believe that just a few years ago I was using a cell phone
to make calls instead of texting, updating social media, and
obsessively sling-shotting red angry birds across the screen. Technology is fun.

But I have a theory as to why we're so preoccupied with technology. It's more than just fun; we're hardwired for it. Something
in our God-imaged nature thrives on making new discoveries and
inventing new widgets. This is one aspect of our human nature
that sets us apart from the animal kingdom. It's our ability to
innovate, to invent a new thing, or to look at an old thing from a
new angle. And you may be shocked to learn that this propensity
toward human innovation is why you have a Bible to read in so
many formats today.

THE GREATEST STORY EVER SOLD

Most people have heard that the Bible is the best-selling book
of all time. But did you know that the Bible has enjoyed a rich

history at the frontiers of publishing technology for almost two thousand years? It's true.

In addition to the written copies of the Scriptures in scroll format, second-century Christians embedded biblical scenes in mosaic tiles on their floors and in the walls of their catacombs and their stone coffins called "sarcophagi."[2] This sort of artistic and symbolic expression was state of the art in the ancient world.

By the second century Christians got tired of carrying around a satchel full of New Testament scrolls. So they began to use the papyrus codex—the precursor to the modern book. These edge-bound papyrus books were so popular with Christians throughout the ancient world that the use of scrolls as a stationery became obsolete by the sixth century.[3]

Then came stained-glass windows in the seventh century. These windows were more than just ornate decorative pieces. They told biblical stories to the illiterate masses. They illustrated scenes from Scripture in order to communicate to those who couldn't read and weren't allowed to own a personal copy of the Bible.[4]

But the "Big Bang" of the Bible industry came in the fifteenth century: Gutenberg's printing press (AD 1455). Gutenberg created a machine with floating type that would allow him to print Bibles faster and more consistently than handwritten manuscripts.[5] With this newfangled machine he could print a whopping ten copies of the Bible a day. This printing revolution set into motion the Reformation, which was largely an effort to get the Bible and other religious tracts into the hands of the common people.

...THAN YOU CAN SHAKE A STICK AT

Fast-forward to the media revolution of our time. The modern believer can store an entire theological library on a smartphone. Today's gadget-savvy Christian has access to Bible apps and software delivered through mind-boggling technology. And sales of the "Good Book" are up, easily exceeding half a billion dollars annually.[6]

This is why the statistics on biblical illiteracy in America are so jarring. Researchers found that the majority of Christians do not know their Scriptures.[7] In fact, the Pew Research organization discovered that atheists and Mormons know the Bible better than the typical evangelical believer.[8]

The church is facing a collapse in theological competence, but not because we don't have access to the Bible. And it's not because we have failed to take advantage of the technologies of our day. We are living in an age of ubiquitous access to Scripture and study tools. We're swimming in technology, and we're saturated with product.

Jesus told the leaders in His day, "You diligently study the Scriptures because you think that by them you possess eternal life. These are the Scriptures that testify about me, yet you refuse to come to me to have life" (John 5:39–40). Notice Jesus said that the Scripture *testifies about Him*. It should lead us to Him. It isn't that the Pharisees had failed to do their homework. And it isn't that Jesus had anything against knowledge growth. I'm sure Jesus set the grade curve in the *bet sefer* synagogue school in Galilee.[9] Jesus demonstrated on multiple occasions that He possessed unrivaled knowledge of the Scriptures.

Now the Pharisees, prominent political-religious leaders in Jesus's day, had honed and sharpened their delivery systems.[10] They were custodians of an oral tradition that sought to apply the Scriptures to everyday situations. They had specific jurisprudence for every possible civil and moral scenario. They also had created an educational system that was the envy of their Greco-Roman counterparts.[11] They were the masters of innovating new ways to stay Torah-compliant. Their answer to the spiritual deficits of their day was more schools, more laws, and more religion. These men acted as the strict and priggish schoolmarms of Israel. Guardians of the sacred. Custodians of the rulebook.

When Jesus chastised them for failing to find eternal life in the

Scriptures, He was referring to their reluctance to come to Him as the giver of the Spirit. Just think how effective those leaders would have been had they submitted their great learning and ingenious delivery systems to Jesus the Master. Yet they refused to come to Jesus to have Spirit life. Spirit life is the defining characteristic of God's people in the end times.

Though I am all for inventive ways to get the word out, we simply cannot improve upon certain aspects of our Christian experience. And if we're not careful, we can fall into the same trap that the Pharisees did: sidelining the work of the Spirit in favor of our well-meaning programs and Spirit-less ingenuity.

WHO'S AFRAID OF THE HOLY SPIRIT?

In our day Spirit-less Christianity has embraced a most unusual excuse.

Our capacity to modernize our delivery methods of Scripture has outpaced our passion to engage the God of the sacred text. That's why we're biblically illiterate. As evangelicals, we are awfully excited about the Bible. The endless stream of Bible products that we crank out each year are proof of that. But for some, the text has become an idol as they have replaced a living faith with an undue veneration of the inspired Scriptures. These are the same Scriptures that are supposed to lead us to the source of life—Jesus! William Law put it so well:

> Read whatever chapter of scripture you will, and be ever
> so delighted with it—yet it will leave you as poor, as
> empty and unchanged as it found you unless it has turned
> you wholly and solely to the Spirit of God, and brought
> you into full union with and dependence upon him.[12]

Law wrote those words over two hundred years ago, yet they still ring true today for our spiritually bankrupt, empty, and morally unchanged American church. The contrast between powerless American religion and the first-century church is startling.

Those Christians only had bits and fragments of the New Testament because it hadn't been completed and circulated in its entirety. When Paul preached in cities along the Mediterranean coast, he showed up with a few Old Testament parchments and *the power of the proclaimed gospel of Jesus.* This Spirit-enabled message was the power of God for salvation. The Spirit's power was demonstrated in everything from miraculous signs to the radical transformation of lost men. Before the first- and second-century Christians had a completed Bible, they had Jesus present by the Spirit.

Unfortunately the gospel can morph into a message about the Bible instead of a message about Jesus. Reflecting on his own experience, New Testament scholar Dan Wallace writes:

> …as a New Testament professor, the [biblical] text is my task—but I made it my God. The text became my idol. Let me state this bluntly: *The Bible is not a member of the Trinity.* One lady in my church facetiously told me, "I believe in the Trinity: the Father, Son, and Holy Bible."[13]

Wallace advocates for a "Christocentric" faith. That is, Christ-centered Christianity—we worship the *God of the Bible, not the Bible.* Wallace refers to the worship of the text as "bibliolatry," which is an undue veneration of the Christian Scriptures. Bibliolatry is actually a harmful innovation that diminishes the power of the gospel of Jesus because it replaces our passion for the *author* of the text with a devotion to the *apparatus*—the text itself. Wallace continues:

> The net effect of such bibliolatry is a depersonalization of God. Eventually, we no longer relate to him. God becomes the object of our investigation rather than the Lord to whom we are subject. The vitality of our religion gets sucked out. As God gets dissected and trisected…our stance changes from "I trust in" to "I believe that."[14]

Bibliolatry is, in fact, an odd but predictable permutation of the gospel that has rendered the church powerless in our day.

AN UNWELCOMED INNOVATION

But before a twinge of guilt fires across your synapses, it will comfort you to know that this temptation to innovate the Spirit out of a job has been going on since the first century. And it has always clothed itself in the attire of good old-fashioned religious devotion.

Paul received a report about the church in Galatia that cut him deep. "My dear children," Paul wrote, "for whom I am again in the pains of childbirth until Christ is formed in you" (Gal. 4:19). Can you hear the angst in the apostle's words? Paul often warned his faith children with misty eyes (Acts 20:19, 31; 2 Cor. 2:4). But the situation in Galatia was particularly disturbing. They were attempting to finish in the flesh what God had started by His Spirit. Their response to the Spirit was, in effect, "Thanks for forgiveness and regeneration. We'll take it from here." This error was serious enough to warrant a letter in response. Pecking and scratching away at the papyrus with his reed pen, Paul burned up the page with scathing words intended to reorient the deceived Galatians:

> I would like to learn just one thing from you: Did you receive the Spirit by observing the law, or by believing what you heard? Are you so foolish? After beginning with the Spirit, are you now trying to attain your goal by human effort?...Does God give you his Spirit and work miracles among you because you observe the law, or because you believe what you heard?
> —GALATIANS 3:2–3, 5

Paul discovered that his rivals, the Judaizers, had infiltrated the church in Galatia (Gal. 5:1). These men were a Jewish faction that broke off from the church in Jerusalem. In addition to believing in Jesus, these false teachers insisted that the Gentiles needed to complete their conversion by embracing the marks of the Judaic covenant: circumcision, kosher diet, and hallowed events on the Jewish calendar. Basically the Judaizers were trying to add these Jewish identity markers to God's message of grace. And the Galatian Christians had bought in.

But Paul would not stand for their innovations to his gospel. Paul wrote with the intensity of a flustered parent who sought to save his Galatian children from the cult of Jesus plus...

ANOTHER GOSPEL

Paul pleaded with the rural church in Galatia to abandon novelty and to resist the marketplace of ideas that had replaced his deep Spirit-gospel with a shallow, watery message of Jesus plus something else. His letter to them opened with a *bang!*—a clever play on the Greek word for "other." "I marvel that you are turning away so soon from Him who called you into the grace of Christ, to a different [Gk. *heteros*] gospel, which is not another [Gk. *allos*]" (Gal. 1:6–7, NKJV).[15] A stinging salvo meant to confront the wrongheaded ritualism that had invaded their faith.

Paul reminded them how they received the Spirit in the first place. It was by believing the message of Christ crucified and resurrected. This belief is neither schmaltzy sentiment, nor is it the robotic response of a soul being coerced by an unseen force. The faith that justified them in God's sight was simply a Spirit-enabled reach for the life preserver of grace. Paul's message was a simple and uncomplicated call to life in the Spirit by faith.

A FAITH LIFT

My enduring picture of simple, uncomplicated faith comes from a fairly traumatic experience in my childhood.

My dad's best friend, Jim, had these two mean dogs. Every time we went to his house, the mutts would explode out of their grungy doghouses to devour me. Barking. Frothing. Enraged as if someone had seasoned their dog food with gunpowder. For some reason the dogs were chained between the driveway and the front door of Jim's old house. Each time I'd freeze with fear looking down that long walkway to Jim's porch. When you're six years old, every dog looks like a ferocious man-eater.

I knew I'd never make it to Jim's front step without a lift.

I'd stand there beside the old blue truck with my arms raised crying, "Daddy! Hurry! Pick me up, Daddy!" My dad would scoop me up and plant me on his shoulders, carrying me all the way to the front door. The savage beasts would jump all over Dad, and I could hear them snarling and snapping at my ankles.

It never once occurred to me to worry about Dad's safety. Not one time did I ever doubt my father's resolve or his competence. I knew when I was on Daddy's shoulders that those barking demons in dog fur couldn't touch me. In the same way, faith is what happens when you let go and let God lift you—when you cry out and rest in His competence, His power, His ability to get you to your destination.

Paul reminded the Galatians, "Because you are sons, God sent the Spirit of his Son into our hearts, the Spirit who calls out, 'Abba, Father'" (Gal. 4:6). Now, the word *Abba* isn't a reference to some ghostly white disco band from the seventies with golden tufts of hair. In Jesus's day *Abba* was an Aramaic term of affection that no rabbi would ever dare apply to God.[16] No rabbi except for Jesus and Paul, that is. The term was considered far too informal to address the Almighty.

Jesus did not come to offer us a new rulebook. The Christian faith wasn't and isn't a new religious system with its own set of rules and rites and sacred to-do lists. Fortunately for the Galatians, Paul didn't have to start from square one. The Spirit had already been poured out among them in power because they trusted in the message they had heard, not because of their fastidious compliance to all the religious add-ons.

The Spirit enables us to reach out for rescue—God's grace lifts us above that which would surely devour and wreck us.

Paul insisted that the Galatians received the Spirit by faith in the gospel message and nothing else. They had left behind the old and had embraced the new. Since they began in faith—they needed to complete their journey in faith by the Spirit.

When It's Jesus Plus...

Any innovation, no matter how well meaning, to the gospel of grace is an affront to the Spirit's rightful place. In similar fashion to the Galatian Christians so long ago, evangelicals today are tempted to replace the dynamic work of the Spirit with something that looks like fully devoted Christianity because of its righteous commitment to the Book. But often it is just an excessive and unwarranted fixation with the Scripture rather than the source—the Spirit who inspired the text. The task of the worshipper is to read *through* the Bible *to* the God of the Bible—the living Word.[17] The irony here is that when we practice reading through Scripture to the God of Scripture, we'll actually become better Bible students and we'll be more enthusiastic about the sacred text. Love for God's truth is the by-product of passionate love for God. Jack Deere stated:

> It is hard to read a book every day that tells how God supernaturally intervenes in the daily lives of his children, and yet see no practical relevance for these supernatural phenomena in our present experience....The Bible is more than a theological treatise. It is a guide to dynamic encounters with the God of wonders. The Bible was given to us that we might hear God's voice and respond to that voice with life-changing faith.[18]

The truth is, we have all the Bible we're ever going to have or ever need. What the church so desperately needs in this hour is a biblically informed *experience*—a passionate friendship with the living God of Scripture who sets hearts, lips, hands, and ears ablaze with His presence. The Spirit wants to continue the work in us that He has started by faith. He wants to give us a dynamic and biblically informed faith. And whenever we are tempted to innovate the Spirit out of a job, we must remember the message to the Galatians and its application to us.

When it's Jesus plus your denominational distinctives, you're drifting away from the moorings of grace.

When we obscure Jesus with our convoluted religious systems, we bar the way for others and we stunt our spiritual growth.

When our doctrine of the Trinity looks more like "the Father, Son, and Scripture" than Father, Son, and Spirit, we've missed the point dramatically.

No Proxy for the Passion

I'm glad I have a smartphone and an electronic tablet with which to read the Bible in every version imaginable. I'm also pleased that many churches, including my own, work hard to contextualize the gospel to our community. This often involves creative expressions of the gospel to the receiving culture, which I wholeheartedly affirm. My sincere hope is that you have taken advantage of the rich resources that are available in print and online. Innovation is a good thing. But not when it comes to the substance of God's gospel. The gospel that the church preached to the Roman Empire was not that God had given them a Bible. It was that God had given them His Son to die on a cross, and the Son had given us the Spirit by faith. Now, we know of all that because we have a Bible, and we should be grateful for it. The Scriptures are able to make us wise for this salvation, but they are not, in and of themselves, that salvation.

Likewise we may devise helpful tools to give expression to our passion, but there's no stand-in for the passion itself. There are no additives or substitutes for the work among us that only God's presence can accomplish. There is and never will be an app for that.

3
ANOTHER ONE
We've reduced the Spirit to His manifestations.

> The Spirit comes with the tenderness of a
> true friend and protector to save, to heal, to
> teach, to counsel, to strengthen, to console.
> The Spirit comes to enlighten the mind
> first of the one who receives him, and then,
> through him, the minds of others as well.[1]
> —CYRIL OF JERUSALEM—

IT'S HEARTBREAKING TO watch siblings battle over a deceased parent's estate. Communication lines go down and walls go up. The same kids who played dress up, built backyard forts, or marched across the kitchen floor with army men are now sworn mortal enemies. Grown children who share their parent's DNA and share a grief over loss and love must now divvy up the leftovers—the personal effects of the departed. Studies show that estate battles are the number-one reason for siblings not speaking in America.

Lost in the shuffle of all this is the memory of the deceased. While the adult children battle, the very existence of the dearly departed is cheapened into a few legacy items—some china, a stack of old letters, and a drafty house. The parents who were once living, thinking beings are now reduced to the sum of their manifestations—a ledger and a lawsuit.

And memories that ought to be precious can become atomized in the process.

Gone forever.

Perhaps no subject in the Christian church is more divisive or has caused more tension than the matter of spiritual gifts. Brothers and sisters in Christ who share the same supernatural DNA, the same resurrection power coursing through their spiritual veins, will divide over which gifts have passed away with the apostles and which gifts belong to the church today. But we must be careful that we don't destroy relationships and Christian unity over the issue of Jesus's *stuff*. As believers, we should resist our tendency to divide over expressions of Spirit activity, sacrificing the bonds of peace over who gets to be more precise about the issue. Paul taught that we are all baptized into the same Spirit (Eph. 4), meaning we're one family. So long as we worship the same Jesus and have the same Spirit, then unity should be our overriding value (vv. 1–4).

In the previous chapters we established that sidelining the Holy Spirit is not a good idea. There is no substitute for a living, passionate faith in Jesus, energized by the Spirit of God and informed by God's authoritative Word. In this chapter we'll address the opposite end of the spectrum. It is the tendency of some to place an excessive emphasis on the bells and whistles—the miraculous effects of the Spirit.

Those of us who have experienced a dramatic deliverance, healing, or a spiritual gift must remember that the Holy Spirit is not the sum of His miraculous manifestations. A manifestation is a visible expression of an inward reality. Manifestations are the effects of the Spirit moving and speaking in our midst. But the Spirit cannot be reduced to His effects. He is a person who desires to be known in His own right. We must be careful not to lose sight of Him in pursuit of the next charismatic fix. We'll have much to say in later chapters about these manifestations. But before we jump to the expressions of the Spirit in the church, we must establish that the Spirit is a person who thinks, feels, responds, and accompanies us through the badlands of life.

A Rowdy House Church

No church was more gifted and yet more afflicted with character issues than the rowdy Corinthians. All indications are that the Corinthian church was one of the most exciting but tragic churches in the ancient world. The reasons for this were numerous.

First, the city of Corinth was a place of rampant sexual sin.

The depraved moral climate of Corinth clearly affected the church. Though they had embraced the more spectacular gifts of God's Spirit in their midst, the Corinthian believers had not fully broken with the reckless self-indulgence of Corinthian culture. As Gordon Fee has observed, "Although they were the Christian church in Corinth, an inordinate amount of Corinth was yet in them."[2] So they tolerated, for example, a young man who was having sexual relations with his stepmother (1 Cor. 5:1). Paul wrote them to expel the rebellious man in hopes of saving him in the end.

Second, Corinth was an epicenter of cultic activity.

Corinth was rich in temples to false deities.[3] The city was home to some of the most popular cults in the ancient world, such as Poseidon, Aphrodite, and worshippers of Isis.[4] All of these cults practiced charismatic phenomena—that is, they believed the enlightened members were gifted with supernatural abilities given to them by their deities.[5] Paul mentioned that many of the Corinthian believers had been active pagans before their conversion (1 Cor. 12:2). This means that new believers likely imported into church life a hunger for ecstatic supernatural experience.

Third, Corinth was a hotbed for hero worship.

Corinthian citizens worshipped renowned heroes tied to their athletic enterprise.[6] This hero worship translated into the Corinthian believers' susceptibility to "super-apostle" devotion (2 Cor. 11:23). The church was divided into factions. Some were fans of Peter, some were devotees to Apollos, and others were waving banners in favor of Paul. Still others were following charlatans who claimed an elite apostleship. Paul forbade this shallow expression of hero worship in the church. His message was clear: leaders who vaunt themselves as "it-on-a-stick" are misguided and in danger of being harshly judged by God (1 Cor. 3:10–15). Shallow allegiances were entirely out of place for God's chosen people. Neither Apollos nor Paul were anything. The credit of their transformation belonged to God alone (v. 6).

The churches in Corinth had overemphasized the manifestations of the Spirit and were undervaluing character formation (1 Cor. 13:1–8). They fancied themselves as spiritually advanced, yet Paul had to tamp down on their pride by calling them "spiritual nurslings" (1 Cor. 3:1–3).

MISUSE, DISUSE, OR PROPER USE?

Without question Paul had to crack down on those rowdy Corinthians. Most biblical commentators gravitate toward this observation. Yet we should also note that God's Spirit was *allowing* things to get rowdy in Corinth. At no time did Paul actually call into question the *manifestations themselves*. Indeed, one of the spiritual abilities given to these believers was the gift of discernment, which helped them to distinguish between Christian and cultic manifestations. It is true that Paul had to prescribe self-control, organization, and intervals of silence for their raucous worship services. But before we judge them, we need to remember that the Spirit was showing up and energizing their worship.

Yes, they needed to bring some symmetry and order to it.

Yes, the spirit of the prophets needed to become subject to the prophets.

No doubt they needed to replace their fractured environment with collaboration and unity.

Of course, their ecstatic outbursts needed strategic placement.

But Paul never called into question the *phenomena itself*—just their reckless application of it. Misuse doesn't call for disuse but calls for proper use. Paul's corrective measures didn't entail abandonment of the Spirit's work among them.

SCRAMBLING TO KEEP UP

Though there have been many of these types of outpourings over the centuries, the church today is seeing a literal resurgence of the Spirit's work. But in America? Not so much.

The vast majority of these outpourings are happening overseas. In his thought-provoking book entitled *The Kingdom Triangle: Recover the Christian Mind, Renovate the Soul, Restore the Spirit's Power*, philosopher J. P. Moreland noted that much of the explosive missions and evangelism taking place in the third-world region today is "intimately connected to signs and wonders as expressions of the love of the Christian Father-God, the lordship of his Son, and the power of his Spirit and his Kingdom."[7] He observes that while Christians in America may find miracle stories hard to take, the Holy Spirit seems to be alive and well, working powerfully to advance the gospel around the world.

The early Christians didn't just hear the gospel; they saw its power to transform lives (1 Cor. 4:20). Speaking of this, Moreland writes, "An important arena in which this power is manifested is in healing, demonic deliverance, and divine interactions through dreams, visions, words of knowledge/wisdom, and prophetic utterances."[8] While American Christendom is quickly becoming conquered by the godless worldview of secular society, God's Spirit is fully engaged in a powerful way, taking new ground in third-world regions. And church leaders in the third world are scrambling to keep up with what God is doing.

When the Spirit was poured out at Pentecost, the hundred or so believers in existence hadn't strategized to create a network of "house churches" in order to assimilate the crowds of thousands. They didn't have time to create systems and structures and networks—at least not until after the fact. The Spirit simply blew through their town and has been blowing from town to town ever since. Those early believers then found themselves feverishly working to arrange their lives according to the Spirit's work. Today much of the third world is clambering to assimilate and train believers who have been transformed by God's presence in powerful ways.

I remember when the Spirit blew into my town and into my life. And I have been scrambling to catch up with Him ever since.

THE UNFLAPPABLE SAM

As a kid my favorite Dr. Seuss story was *Green Eggs and Ham*. I loved how the main character repeatedly resists the attempts of Sam-I-Am to get him to try something new. But the unflappable Sam pursues the narrator and finally gets him to try the strange green eggs and ham. The main character's eyes widen, a grin stretches across his face—and to his surprise he discovers that he *does* like the slimy green eggs and ham. The lesson was clear: something you avoided because it looked weird might actually turn out to be amazing, even life changing.

Years after I was baptized in water, I recommitted my life to Jesus in dramatic fashion. My mom started attending a church in Richmond, Virginia, where the people seemed enthusiastic about their faith. The first time I visited that church they were singing choruses accompanied by a band and an orchestra, all with hands raised praising God. I left that service and asked my mom, "How come the pastor never answered those people's questions? They sat there for half the service with their hands raised."

My mom laughed and explained that this was a posture of worship. Though I sensed something different in that place, I was confused by all the singing and hand raising and the excitement.

In fact, I was very wary of the Spirit people with whom my mom and friends had become associated. The Spirit had ignited a passion for Jesus in them that I couldn't ignore. But, like Sam with the green eggs and ham, I initially resisted something that looked odd to me. I was reluctant to dive in, probably still smarting from my post-baptism spanking. But these people weren't kooks. They were educated, levelheaded Christians who appeared to love God. And though I was cautious at first, the flame of their devotion drew me in.

I WOULD NOT, COULD NOT PRAY LIKE THAT!

Though I was recommitted to Jesus, my growth was slow due to the inertia of old habits. I couldn't clean up my filthy mouth, and I couldn't stop lusting after teenage girls. I was timid about sharing my faith, and I couldn't stop my violent outbursts. I was saved and committed. But frankly, I felt like a mall cop—I had my badge and my Segway, but no gun.

I was hungry for more of God, but what these people were serving up seemed strange to me. The Spirit people I had become associated with were interesting. They had experienced the presence of God in ways that made me uncomfortable, especially during our prayer meetings.

"No way!" was my first response. "I would not, could not pray like *that!*"

But I kept hanging out with my eccentric friends anyway, because they had a passion and a zeal for God that I desired. I wanted to love Jesus the way they did. I wanted their fiery devotion—but I have to admit—I didn't have it.

In one of those prayer meetings my good friend Welford walked across the prayer circle and touched my chest. It was as if he'd cracked open a door in a burning house and the backdraft consumed me! I blew the roof off that room praying molten words from heaven. I was so profoundly transformed by God's power in that moment that it altered the direction of my life. The supernatural God had invaded my space with His transforming presence. And I couldn't deny it.

THE HELP

I became eager for more of God. But soon after, my desire for God mutated into a rapacious hunger for more miraculous manifestations. I became hooked on the attending phenomena of Spirit life. This sent me into a "super-disciple" phase, where I thought I had to fast and pray with monastic fervor in order to obtain more of God in my life. Really, I was after more of God's stuff.

Over the next two years I had subtly shifted from being focused on the God of transforming presence to spiritual gifts. The Spirit of God, who was supposed to be an "ever-present help in trouble" (Ps. 46:1), was now just "the help." The same pride that had gripped the gifted Corinthians so long ago now had its mitts on me. And the results of this lopsided emphasis on gifts versus the God of the gifts were predictable. Like the Corinthians, I had character issues, was divisive and pugnacious, and practiced unwarranted devotion to my super-spiritual heroes. My theory of spiritual formation revolved entirely around words of knowledge, prophecy, visions, and an obsession with casting out demons. But all the dreams, miracles, and exorcisms in the world couldn't take the place of an intimate walk with the Spirit through obedience and faith.

I also made the critical error of trying to make sure that people experienced God the same way that I had. I thought *my* encounter was the normative experience for the Christian life. My brush with the supernatural was the grid through which I judged everyone else's encounters with God. Like the Corinthians, I thought I was hot stuff, but the truth is that I was becoming an un-spiritual amateur.

ANOTHER ONE

My turning point came when I began to rediscover the *person* of the Holy Spirit. I had gone off to college and had begun to establish a solid foundation in biblical doctrine. This is why a sound footing in theology is so critical to our experience. If all we have is doctrine, then we have no life. But without a solid foundation of biblical teaching, we will misinterpret and misapply our experience of the Spirit, or even be led into error. Our spiritual "house" will be a rickety and flimsy thing. We'll never really get any traction in the Christian life. We'll have lots of heat but not much light.

As I studied the Gospel of John, I came to realize that Jesus's promise to send the disciples His Spirit was a comforting assurance of permanency and equivalency. That is, through the Spirit, Jesus would always be with them and would continue to advocate on their behalf. Somehow, mysteriously, Jesus is present by the Holy Spirit in the life of the believer. I made several revolutionary shifts in my understanding of Him.

First, I discovered the Spirit was a He, not an it.

Though I would be quick to tell you that the Spirit was the third person of the Godhead, in practice, however, I tended to relate to the Spirit as "raw power" for life, without an acknowledgment of His personhood. Yet the New Testament shows that like Jesus, the Holy Spirit can be grieved (Eph. 4:30), He can be disrespected (Heb. 10:26, 29), He can be blasphemed (Matt. 12:31–32), and He can be lied to (Acts 5:3). In John's Gospel the Holy Spirit tells the truth (John 14:16–26), He advocates for believers (John 14), and Jesus refers to the Spirit with the personal pronoun *Him* and never as *it*. He is the personal, animating power behind the church's activity, and He sustains our life and ministry. He is God's personal, transforming presence.

Second, I discovered the Spirit was my advocate and not just "the help."

Jesus stated that He would send the disciples "another Advocate." The Greek term for "another" is *allos*, which means "another of the same kind."[9] The Spirit is like Jesus. He does what Jesus does and points us to Christ. The word *advocate* is *paracletos* and comes into English as "paraclete." It has been translated in various ways. The primary thrust of the term is "one who appears on another's behalf, mediator, or intercessor."[10] It doesn't mean that He's your personal therapist. It also doesn't mean "helper" in the sense that the Spirit is there to serve your interests or to respond like a trained Labrador every time you whistle. *Paracletos* means "counselor" in the sense of a legal representative, or one who intervenes on your behalf. He takes up your case while prosecuting your enemy. He is your helper in the midst of your trials and persecutions.

Jesus's use of the phrase "another Advocate," then, assumes they already have an advocate and anticipates that the coming Spirit will be a worthy successor.[11] He does what Jesus does. He defends us the way Jesus defended the disciples. He turns the tables on the world and convicts them of sin and convinces them of righteousness. He also authorizes the disciples to minister to the world in power, the same way Jesus was empowered by the Spirit. The Spirit is another One. He picks up the mantle of Jesus's work.

Third, I discovered Him as the Spirit of truth.

The disciples, according to John's Gospel, appear to misunderstand nearly everything that Jesus says regarding His message and mission until they receive the Spirit at the end of the Gospel. After they receive the Spirit, their eyes are opened and they can understand Jesus's teaching. Jesus was the truth (John 14:6), and the Spirit is a truth teller. He points us back to Jesus's teaching and never contradicts what is written in God's revealed Word.

Once I understood these critical teachings about the Holy

Spirit, my relationship with Him changed. It became, in many ways, more intimate. I still experienced powerful manifestations of the Spirit in church, but my passion for God deepened and matured.

MORE THAN HIS EFFECTS

Jesus could give you a supernatural dream a day, and it wouldn't cure you from bad choices.

Jesus could stock your shelves with an abundance of miracles, and it wouldn't make a dent in your character transformation. There is no such thing as the "gift of integrity." Spirit-formed character is refined and strengthened in the cauldron of trials and difficulty.

He could deliver you from every curse, every oppressive spirit from your past, every tormenting addiction, and it still wouldn't do much to ignite a passionate appetite for God in your spirit. I wonder how many of the people whom Jesus delivered on the hillsides of Galilee later joined the crowd, calling for His crucifixion before Pilate? After you get some deliverance and shake all the demons out of your family tree, you might want to try some good old-fashioned faithfulness and obedience. Jesus wants to deliver you. But He also wants to *disciple* you. He isn't only interested in your charismatic development; He's interested in your character formation.

The Spirit is God's transforming presence in our midst. He was sent in order to continue the work of Jesus through the messianic community—the church. This is precisely why Luke opened the Book of Acts by writing, "In my former book, Theophilus, I wrote about all that Jesus *began to do and to teach*" (Acts 1:1, emphasis added). The statement "all that Jesus began to do and teach" implies that the Book of Acts was a continuation of Jesus's own mission—through the Spirit-empowered church. The Spirit is another One, sent to minister and to continue Jesus's ministry, a ministry of miracles and a ministry of spiritual formation. A ministry of mind-boggling exploits and the ministry of quiet, intimate transformation of heart.

Along the way I had to begin to see the Spirit as so much more than the bells and whistles of supernatural manifestations. He is God's own Spirit come to live in me. He accurately represents Jesus and never garbles messages from the Father. He continues the work of Jesus in us by revealing the truth of His Word and demonstrating His power. We need to be open to His power. But arrogant and strident Christianity is not what God had in mind when He sent us His Spirit.

My hope is that you're beginning to see just how much the Spirit is another One—not the other one. The Spirit has been largely ignored, replaced, and marginalized when He should be central to all that we do as He points us to Jesus. In the next section we'll begin to explore what the Spirit is doing in the church today and how to experience His transforming presence in our lives.

PART TWO
A SIGN BETWEEN THE TIMES
What on earth is the Spirit doing today?

IN-BETWEEN IS A hard place to live. Between the résumé and the job, between promise and fulfillment, between loss and the soul's healing. During these seasons of transition we can find ourselves in a mess of ambiguity.

The Jews in Jesus's day were living between the way things were and the way things were supposed to be. Jesus's countrymen believed in a "two-age" system. The Gentiles—cruel, ruthless, merciless, tawdry pagans—dominated the present age. And they had been in control for a long time. The Jews were convinced that God was going to deliver them from this age through a sudden in-breaking of a new *kingdom* age.

They thought the Messiah, when He finally came, would trounce the Gentiles as David had done the Philistines, like the Hasmonean boys—Judas, Jonathan, and Simon—had done to the Greeks a generation before them (165 BC). The Galileans naturally expected a conqueror who would reestablish the Davidic kingdom forever, ushering in a new age of God's dominion and rule.

This is why Jesus's message of reconciliation for outsiders was so jarring.

His scandalous announcement that He'd come to save those foul and loathsome Gentiles started a riot in His hometown in Nazareth (Luke 4). These are the same Jews who watched their sons and husbands and fathers suspended between earth and sky,

affixed to crosses littering the hillsides in a gruesome display of
Roman brutality.

Outrageous! Appalling!

Jewish messiahs don't reach out to Gentiles—they exact their
vengeance. Israel's...no...*God's* vengeance.

Let's see how this homegrown "Savior" feels about the Gentiles
after He bounces down the bluffs and crags of Nazareth.

The Messiah as a "great light for those in darkness" was not
their vision. Not by a mile.

But Jesus insisted that He was everyone's Christ, not just
theirs. The coming of the Spirit signaled that God's new kingdom
age had broken into our fallen world. And while it didn't put an
end to this age, it did signal that this era—this epoch—is on its
way out. God was gracious enough to send us His Spirit in the
middle of our mess. So we live between the times—between the
old order of things and the day when Jesus will consummate His
kingdom and put an end to the corrupt governments and the
crooked enterprises of men.

Part 2 will address what the Spirit is doing in this in-between
time. Now that we've established that He is a person who is
indispensible to our lives, we want to focus on what He's up to.
We'll discover that life in the Spirit should be characterized by
the attending phenomena, or the manifestations of the Spirit. A
manifestation is a visible expression of an inward reality. It is this
aspect of the Spirit's work that can sometimes make us uncomfortable. The Spirit wants to equip us in this already-but-not-yet
kingdom so that we may serve others in His resurrection power
and so that we may be formed into the image of Jesus.

4
TREASURE IN A CHIPBOARD CASE
The Spirit is our inheritance.

> Part of receiving an inheritance is that you have
> to know it's there in order to receive it. You
> can be sent letters about it (the Bible), but if
> you don't open them up and read them, you
> won't know what it is you've inherited. And
> you won't know what to do to possess it.[1]
> —STORMIE OMARTIAN—
> *Lead Me, Holy Spirit*

My FRIENDS STEVE and Barb once sent out a postcard
inviting the neighbors to the church where they pastored.
The postcard read, "Less Nod, More God." The direct mailer
didn't get much traction, but the creative phrase has always stuck
with me.

By all accounts, we live in a bored nation.[2] Did you know that
91 percent of all young adults say they experience boredom regularly?[3] A full 70 percent of us frequently use our cell phones
to stave off boredom.[4] Surprisingly, many Christians wonder if
heaven will be boring. It seems as though Isaac Asimov's fear
has seeped into our collective consciousness: "For whatever the
tortures of hell, I think the boredom of heaven would be even
worse."[5]

Boredom is the scourge of a culture that is preoccupied with
self-interests. Indeed, our founding documents supply a guarantee

for the pursuit of life, liberty, and happiness. Freedom from tyranny and the chance to pursue one's destiny are the hallmark of the American experience. At the time our founding documents were written, the only alternative to the right to pursue happiness and personal freedom was vassalage to some unworthy despot. In a sense, the potential for personal happiness and satisfaction is our national birthright. It's our brand. In and of itself, there's nothing wrong with that.

Yet the American experience has been hijacked by the pursuit of self. In his book *Still Bored in a Culture of Entertainment: Rediscovering Passion and Wonder*, Rich Winter documents the major contributors to boredom in our nation over the last two centuries: 1) the emergence of the cult of leisure, and 2) the decline of a self-less Christian ethos.[6] Our contemporary society has made it possible for us to spend our lives pursuing our hobbies and interests. This has resulted in a kind of disposable culture: Don't like that dull marriage? Then trade it in for an exciting new one. Don't want the onerous burden of a job? Then by all means become a freeloading parasite to society. Are the responsibilities of kids and bills cramping your style? Then swap them out for a lifestyle that fits *your* needs.

Most Americans have bought the lie that our highest priority in life is our immediate gratification. It is hedonism disguised in the respectable apparel of personal ambition and self-realization. But at the moment we bow to this idol of self-actualization, we become subjects to an awful tyrant. Ironically we proclaim ourselves "free" from behind the steel rods of our self-made prisons. We declare ourselves "enlightened" when we are really the dumbest of fools. We are thin, gaunt, emaciated shadows of our garden selves. We have the faint likeness of heaven but not its presence. And more good news: new technologies designed to enhance our "sense experience" are rushing into existence and are being forced into the service of this bored-out-of-its-mind, over-indulged self-god.

No God

The downside to a culture where the unbridled pursuit of happiness is married to unlimited sensate technologies is that we have become inoculated from God and thus to wonder. We are lurching toward oblivion on autopilot. Numb. Dazed. Bored stiff in the middle of a verdant garden well stocked with the miraculous—a world dazzling and beautiful but damaged and broken. Like a defaced Rembrandt, or Michelangelo's sculpture of David, marred and splotched with graffiti. Perhaps we are the ones who have been damaged. Our sight has been diminished. No longer can we see the glory of God in a glorious world. We are irked by the resplendent, annoyed by the extraordinary.

This is just part of our fallen human nature.

For example, I remember the first time I ever flew on a jet plane. All of my senses were alive during that first flight. My pulse quickened as the plane taxied and picked up speed. My stomach leaped as the jet climbed skyward. I took forty pictures of the tops of clouds that day. A century before the automobile, people thought if you travelled at 60 mph you'd fly apart. And there I was, hurtling through the air in a metal tube at 500 mph, six miles high. The thought of sleeping through that seemed crazy to me. No way!

That was twenty-five years ago. Now when I fly, *smwock*—in go the earplugs, back goes the seat, down goes the Dramamine, and it's snoozeville all the way. I'm sure I'll rediscover the wonder of flight if and when I ever take my first commercial trip to outer space. But soon after my tenth trip outside the thermosphere, I'll be too busy to be awestruck by space. I'll have more important things to do such as typing away on my holographic keyboard.

And so I bounce from one conquered hill to the next. And every hill reminds me that the pursuit is over, and so I must cue up another finish line. We spend our lives contriving new challenges so that we can stay interested. Pretty soon I'll think a smartphone is the dumbest thing I've ever heard of. I'll wonder how we ever used those archaic little touch screens. Though we are wired for innovation, it's all meaningless without God at the center of it.

The cure for a bored, overindulged life is God. Knowing and seeing the value of the Spirit deposited in our hearts is the key to revving up a wonder-less existence. We can see God's creation with fresh eyes when the Spirit is present. We're less likely to nod off and miss the point of life the more we allow God's Spirit to be at the center of our endeavors and the focal point of our passions.

We need a bona fide epiphany, a sudden in-breaking of the Spirit of wisdom and revelation. The Spirit is our first inheritance. We were made to be filled, transformed, and surrounded by His presence. Everything about a fish's life—catching food, mating, pitching and darting with the school—can only make sense when he is surrounded and engulfed with water. And nothing about our lives—nothing else we were born to do—makes sense until we are deluged by the Spirit, until we live and move and have our being in Him, our glorious inheritance in the saints.

Just as the pursuit of life, liberty, and happiness is the American birthright, so too is the Spirit the inheritance, the heritage of the believer.

In this chapter we'll tease out what it means for the Spirit to be our inheritance. We'll discover that the Spirit enables us to know God and to discover the incomparable power of resurrection life. Paul told the Ephesian Christians:

> Having believed, you were marked in him with a seal, the promised Holy Spirit, who is a deposit guaranteeing our inheritance until the redemption of those who are God's possession....I keep asking that the God of our Lord Jesus Christ, the glorious Father, may give you the Spirit of wisdom and revelation, so that you may know him better. I pray also that the eyes of your heart may be enlightened in order that you may know the hope to

which [God] has called you, the riches of his glorious
inheritance in the saints.

—Ephesians 1:13–14, 17–18

The Spirit had made them participants in God's holy family,
and Paul prayed that God would enlighten them—open their
eyes to the rich and full life of the Spirit. But how often do
we walk around with our eyes glued shut to the fullness of the
Spirit's inheritance? How often are we unaware of the value of
the One whom God has placed within us? The Spirit wants to
take off our blinders and rev up our humdrum lives. My friends
Steve and Barb were right: more God—less nod.

Know God

Fullness of the Spirit starts with knowing God. Paul prayed that
the Ephesians would be given the Spirit of wisdom and revelation, that they would know God better (Eph. 1:17). And knowing
God is a fundamentally intelligible thing. It isn't rocket science.
That is, since we were creatures made for Him, loving Him
should be second nature for us. Knowing God through the Spirit
comes naturally as we consider the evidence for God in nature
and through direct revelation of the Spirit to our spirit. The first
thing the Spirit does in this in-between era is to reveal the God
of wonders to us.

We know God through indirect evidence.

Jesus said to the rabbinic pundits embedded in His crowd,
"But so that you may know that the Son of Man has authority
on earth to forgive sins..." (Matt. 9:6). Then He told the lame
man to get up and walk. In other words, Jesus called their attention to *the evidence*. On another occasion Jesus challenged the
pious Jews that if they couldn't believe His lofty claims, then they
should at least believe the irrefutable evidence of His miracles
(John 10:36–38).

After Jesus rose from the dead, Scripture says that He showed the disciples "many convincing proofs" in order to confirm their faith (Acts 1:3). Additionally, Luke described Paul's primary method of evangelism as proving from the Scriptures that Jesus was the Christ as he often "reasoned with them" (Acts 17:2). When Paul made his case to the Romans, he appealed to the obvious revelation of God in nature (Rom. 1:19).

Our knowledge of God is based in evidence though it is not bound by evidence. And the Spirit is the key to this. Paul stated, "But people who aren't spiritual can't receive these truths from God's Spirit. It all sounds foolish to them and they can't understand it, for only those who are spiritual can understand what the Spirit means" (1 Cor. 2:14, NLT). Paul was referring to the revelation the Spirit gives us concerning the truth. The first thing the Spirit enables us to do is to recognize God through the miraculous: the effects of creation and supernatural signs and wonders. The Spirit gives you new eyes so that you can "wise up" to God's activity. This is the "Spirit of wisdom" that Paul prayed the Ephesians would know.

We know God through direct revelation.

Philosopher William Lane Craig is the greatest living defender of the Christian faith today, having debated prolific atheists all over the world. Dr. Craig presents a cumulative case for God's existence based on the evidence from philosophy, science, and religious knowledge. Yet Dr. Craig maintains that it is primarily the witness of the Spirit that convinces men of the truth.[7] *There is no greater evidence for God than God Himself.*

This is why Paul told the Ephesians that he prayed that they would receive the Spirit of wisdom *and revelation*, that they may know God better (Eph. 1:17). Referring to the Holy Spirit, Jesus promised that rivers of living water would flow from within the believer (John 7:37–38). The Spirit's internal witness is veridical and phenomenological, meaning it's a real and direct experience of God's Spirit.

Our first priority as believers is to know God intellectually, experientially, and personally. Our inheritance as believers is the knowledge of God through the evidence in creation and the direct revelation of the Holy Spirit. The Spirit gives us the wisdom to see God's fingerprints in creation and gives a personal disclosure of His truth. Before the Spirit does anything else in our lives, He opens the eyes of our hearts that we may know God. Knowing God is the only cure to an otherwise flaccid, rhythmless, uninspired existence.

KNOW THE HOPE

G. K. Chesterton once stated, "Hope is the power of being cheerful in circumstances we know to be desperate."[8] After knowing their God through the Spirit of wisdom and revelation, Paul prayed that the Ephesians would know their hope (Eph. 1:18). Hope is a confident expectation of better days in the face of evidence to the contrary. And the Spirit-redeemed heart has an amazing capacity for hope.

Paul put it this way to Pastor Titus: "We wait for the blessed hope—the glorious appearing of our great God and Savior, Jesus Christ" (Titus 2:13). Jesus Himself is our hope. When He appears, He will complete His work by transforming us into an incorruptible state (1 Cor. 15). And the Spirit was the key to this confident expectation. Paul wrote, "By faith we eagerly await through the Spirit the righteousness for which we hope" (Gal. 5:5). The Spirit gives us courage in the midst of a messed-up world. Paul's prayer for the Ephesians was that the Spirit would give them a confident expectation of better days, a hope that is imperishable and impenetrable. It is a hope that cannot be diminished by the onslaught of trying events—broken promises, temporary failure, or attacks from the enemy. This Spirit-inspired hope is part of our birthright as believers, and it is foreign to those who do not have the Spirit.

KNOW YOUR INHERITANCE

The key to this hope is our inheritance—the very presence of God in our hearts. Paul used the metaphor of a "deposit," or an installment, guaranteeing the future completion of a transaction that starts now (Eph. 1:18). It's as if the Spirit is the earnest payment, ensuring the final transformation that Jesus is holding for us in escrow. And the Spirit is the agent of our transformation—partially now and fully then.

Back when my wife and I were renters, we would occasionally house-sit for some friends who lived in an upscale gated community. Our friends recommended us to their neighbor, Dr. Roberts. Dr. Roberts was retired and his house looked like a sprawling mansion to me. We were glad to help him out and agreed to be freeloading squatters for a few weeks.

One of the items on my checklist for Dr. Roberts's house was to go around and lock up all the windows and double-check all the doors. So after dinner the first night, I made my rounds and found my way down to the basement. I flipped on the light switch and peeked through the basement door window—and that's when I saw it. I spotted an old chipboard guitar case on top of a large pile of random stuff in the middle of the room. Chipboard is nothing more than painted fiberboard or cardboard. You typically don't put an expensive solid wood spruce and rosewood guitar in a flimsy case like that. Chipboard cases are reserved for your fifty-dollar plywood guitar. Not a handcrafted work of fine luthiery.

So I assumed whatever was inside Dr. Roberts's old case wasn't of much value. But being a guitar guy, I just had to peek.

I popped the latches and lifted the lid and could not believe what I was looking at. There, inside, was a vintage pre-war Martin guitar in fabulous condition. The Martin Company invented the steel string acoustic guitar. I knew enough to know that the gem inside of the chipboard case was worth somewhere around ten thousand dollars to the right collector.

I called Dr. Roberts to ask him some questions about the old treasure.

"Do you know what it's worth?"

"Well. No. Honestly, Jeff, I don't know anything about guitars, and that one has just been in the family for a while."

What he said next floored me. "Jeff, how would you like to take that guitar as partial payment for helping out with the place?"

"What? Um. Dr. Roberts, I appreciate that. But this guitar isn't worth a few hundred bucks. It's probably worth thousands of dollars. This guitar is a family heirloom. You'll want to keep something like this in your family and pass it on to your kids someday."

He thought for a moment and replied, "Well. I think you're probably right then."

Jesus told the disciples to wait in Jerusalem until they received the promise of the Father. The Holy Spirit is the promise God made to Abraham to restore the world and set it right. The Spirit is our inheritance (Gal. 3:14, 18). And an inheritance belongs to the children. He is the birthright of those who by faith have embraced the world's true Messiah—Jesus.

Before Jesus, the promise of resurrection was thought to only be for the Jews. No pagan believed in bodily resurrection anyway. But unique to Christianity was the teaching that Jesus, the perfect Jew, had already resurrected. The resurrection hope that the Jewish nation believed was their inheritance at the end of the world had already begun in the risen Messiah. He fulfilled their symbols, their sacred structures, and their Scriptures (Matt. 5:17). And now He has summoned the nations to worship Him as the vindicated, resurrected Lord.

But Christians taught that all who were born into this new family by the Spirit, both Jew and Gentile, would participate in this resurrection at the end of the world. So the Spirit is our promise that we have been spliced into the vine (Rom. 9) and that we have received the inheritance of the saints—eternal life with God.

This is why Paul can say to the Ephesians, "For through him we both have access to the Father by one Spirit" (Eph. 2:18). We participate in Israel's hope of future resurrection because we have been made "fellow citizens" being built into a holy temple of the Lord by the Spirit. Our future resurrection is a sure thing. You can bet on it. And God's Spirit vouchsafes that future event. Paul stated that he wanted your eyes to be opened "in order that you may know the hope to which he has called you, the riches of his glorious inheritance in the saints" (Eph. 1:18). The Spirit is the opening act—He's the first installment of our future transformation.

KNOW THE POWER

In addition to knowing the hope that was their inheritance of future salvation, Paul prayed that the Ephesians would know "his incomparably great power for us who believe. That power is like the working of his mighty strength, which he exerted in Christ when he raised him from the dead and seated him at his right hand in the heavenly realms" (Eph. 1:19–20).

Did you catch that? The same power that raised Jesus is available to the believer. It isn't just a future expectation; it's power for the here and now. It's the Spirit's power. This is part of our inheritance in the saints.

I like the way Paul put it to the Corinthian Christians: "But we have this treasure in jars of clay to show that this all-surpassing power is from God and not from us" (2 Cor. 4:7). This treasure, God's Spirit, is housed in a chipboard people—people who often aren't aware that they are carriers of a most contagious and precious thing. This is an unnerving aspect of our redemption—that the third member of the Trinity inhabits such brokenness. Such frail and ruined vessels are we. God wants us to live in the same resurrection power that raised Jesus from the dead.

That power can raise a failing marriage, it can rescue your rebellious children, and it can resurrect your ruined character.

It can heal your body, right your finances, and mend your broken mind.

That power can also give you a supernatural patience to wait in the face of agonizing delays.

The Spirit is the power of God's kingdom to continue Jesus's work in this world—the work of healing, speaking God's truth, and bringing grace to the bedraggled masses of humanity.

An Unruly Sort

When I was a kid, I went to change the bulb in the lamp on my desk, not realizing that the bulb had been broken. I accidentally touched the filament and innards of the broken bulb. I recall briefly feeling as though worms were crawling through my veins at the speed of light. For half a second I couldn't pull my hand away from the lamp. It felt like forever. It had me in its grip. Then I found myself flat on my back. I thought I was going to die. My dad found me on the floor, picked me up, and took me to the living room to keep an eye on me.

I know what power feels like—raw, scorching, knocking-you-on-your-butt kind of power. Power is a good thing when properly harnessed. It can turn on your lights, start your car engine, and get your plane off the runway. Paul's prayer for the church was that they know the incomparable power of God. This untamable and unruly power would flow through their prayers, their symbols, and their worship. We've already established that the Spirit is a person, but make no mistake about it: He is also *the power of God*. Our inheritance doesn't just involve a future hope of resurrection. It is God's power for living now. Our transformation starts in this life.

We live in this tension: As believers, we have inherited a new world, a new power, the Spirit of God Himself. Yet we live in a world that is broken through sin. And contrary to the American ethos, we do not find our significance through unrestrained self-gratification. We find it, rather, as the Spirit enables us to know our God, to grasp the hope of our inheritance, and to live in Christ's power today.

The inheritance is for the children. And the treasure occupies a chipboard people with squeaky joints and rusted latches. That inheritance is the restored presence of God and the restored place for humanity in the Father's household. This is the promise of our transformation. And to all those who believed on Him, to those who received Him, He gave the power—the right, the authority—to become the children of God (John 1:12).

5
CAN YOU HEAR THE SIRENS?
The Spirit convicts and confronts.

The entire world is falling apart because
nobody will admit they are wrong.[1]
—DONALD MILLER—
Blue Like Jazz

I DON'T KNOW WHY my wife and I did this, but the first year we owned our home we made no effort to change the batteries in our smoke alarms. I discovered that when the batteries got low on the disc-shaped alarms, they would sound off a little *chirp*, reminding the homeowner that it was time for a new battery. We spent about a month just ignoring the occasional *chirp* from the alarm in the kitchen. But after a while it was beeping every two minutes.

So I took the smoke alarm off the ceiling, walked downstairs to the basement, and stuck it in the laundry room. That worked for about an hour, until I realized that I could still hear the alarm chirping from every room in the house. Mildly annoyed, I took it out to the garage and stuck it on a shelf. That bought me a solid hour or two before I realized that I could still faintly hear it...

Chirp!

I was starting to lose it.

So I went out to the garage and angrily buried the alarm in a box and covered it with some old guitar magazines. I briefly glanced over to my workbench where I kept my duct tape. But before I spent the next ten minutes entombing the smoke alarm in a cardboard and duct tape sarcophagus, I finally came to my senses.

"*What* am I doing? Why don't I just change the battery?"

Great idea. I fished the alarm back out of the box, replaced the old battery, and popped it back onto the ceiling—no more annoying chirps.

I think both religious people and sinners have something in common. They share the same motivation. They are both trying to cover up the alarms of guilt and shame—one with religious activity and the other through pleasure seeking.

The role of the Spirit is to cut through all the clutter and to dredge up all that stuff that we've buried and hidden away. Only when we come to our senses and admit our guilt can the Spirit begin His work of life transformation.

So Long, Farewell

In Jesus's well-known "farewell speech" as recorded in John's Gospel, He told the disciples that when the Spirit comes, He "will convict the world concerning sin and righteousness and judgment" (John 16:8, ESV). The Spirit's role is to convict us and to bring clarity to our condition. Conviction is what I refer to as "healthy guilt." If you didn't feel a healthy sense of guilt, you'd have no boundaries, no guidelines—nothing to restrain you from moral oblivion. And most everyone has this sense of moral obligation to his neighbor to a degree. Otherwise, civilized societies wouldn't even be possible. God has given us the gift of guilt. It's the gift of feeling bad when we blow it and feeling empathy for the injustices done to our fellow man.

But the Spirit wants to do more than give you some broad moral parameters. His job is to bring you inexorably to one sobering truth—you are a sinner, far from God. Without Jesus you are headed for a Christ-less eternity. This is precisely what the Spirit did on the Day of Pentecost. Droves of Jews were in

Jerusalem to celebrate a religious feast. After Peter spoke up in the power of the Holy Spirit, the presence of God convicted those good religious people: "They were cut to the heart and said to Peter and the other apostles, 'Brothers, what shall we do?'" (Acts 2:37). Without this work of Spirit conviction, we are hopelessly lost. We need the Spirit to convict us, and we need a preacher to tell us what to do with that conviction. Once you know that the Spirit is your inheritance in the saints—once you discover that the key to revving up a dull life is the Spirit of God at the center of it—then you need to know what the Spirit intends to do. He means to bring you to your knees, admitting that you are a sinner before a holy God. Life in the Spirit begins with Spirit conviction.

SIN-SICK HEART

We see some great glimpses of this Spirit conviction in the Gospels. Mark and Luke tell the story about a wealthy man who was racked with conviction. The young man's theology was fine, but he was having a genuine existential crisis. He suspected that something was still missing, despite his pitch-perfect recitation of the Torah (Luke 18:18–21).

"Good Teacher," the young man inquired, "what can I do to be guaranteed resurrection and a place in God's eternal kingdom when it comes to earth?"

The question is shocking because Jews believed their salvation, or resurrection at the end of the age, was guaranteed in their Abrahamic pedigree. No self-respecting Jewish male would question his future resurrection, especially if he was a Torah-observant Jew. And his wealth, in that culture, would have been ample evidence that God had favored him.[2] Jesus's countrymen believed the false notion that material wealth was a sign of inner righteousness and God's favor. The rich man who approached Jesus had every external reason to believe that God had accepted him.

But the young man has a sickness of heart. He's made his

rounds to every other rabbi in town and they've all prescribed the same cure...

"You should just keep obeying Moses's commands and you'll be fine," comes Jesus's reply. Jesus is simply rehearsing what has already been stipulated in the man's fine Jewish education. This is the answer he would have heard from every other instructor. Jesus's answer is a test of responsiveness. Does this young man really want to know the answer? Or does he just want status-quo theology?

"I have, Master," the rich man protests. "I've meticulously followed the commands since I was old enough to recite Torah in the synagogue."

I think Jesus could hear a genuine undercurrent of heartache in the young man's voice. Mark's version makes it clear that "Jesus looked at him and loved him" (Mark 10:21). The local shamans have sold him snake oil. They've taken his money, but all their cures are bogus. He has been told to keep obeying the commands and he'll be good to go. But he knows better. His heart is genuinely sick with sin, and Jesus shows him compassion.

The text says, "Jesus looked at him" (v. 21). I can imagine in a moment like this, it must have been an odd sensation to have Jesus look straight through you as if you were made of glass. Looking into the windows of the man's soul, Jesus locates the cancer that is killing him. He's found what the young man has buried and sealed under layers of religious activity.

Chirp!

"Go and auction off all your prized possessions," Jesus instructs him. "And whatever is left, have a yard sale at your swank villa and get rid of it. Then, sell the villa. Take all the proceeds and distribute it among the poor and the penniless. Then come be My *talmid*—My disciple." (See Luke 18:22–23.) Abandoning all to follow Jesus would instantly address his guilt. It would instantly confront his false belief that his wealth was a sign of inner piety and God's favor.

The cure is on the table, but the young man cannot accept it.

It is exactly what he needs, but not what he expected. He craves expedience. A bandage. But the master prescribes radical surgery. So the young ruler shuffles away in sadness—heartbroken and unable to silence the alarms of conviction.

The point of the story is not that Jesus has something against rich fat cats. Jesus's demand surfaced a self-imposed barrier to the young man's discipleship. Every prospective disciple has a potential barrier—something that comes between the Master and us. For this young man, it was his wealth. And no amount of religious activity could quiet the pain of empty piety. His meticulous devotion to religion hadn't secured for him the righteousness he so desperately sought.

All the religious activity in the world will not cure us. The Spirit's job is to convict the religious of their trust in vaporous, empty externalisms.

BETTER THAN THE RIFFRAFF

Of course, our point of comparison is the wrong object. We like to compare ourselves to others, don't we? The job of the Spirit is to show us, all of us, that we don't measure up, and then to bring us to confession of our sin. Jesus taught this in a powerful parable directed to all those who are "confident of their own righteousness" (Luke 18:9).

Jesus's story is about a Pharisee—a very pious leader—standing at the temple and observing the atonement offerings. The loud and strident Pharisee thanks God that he is not like the riffraff. "Heavenly Father—I'm so glad that I am not a wretch like all these other people..."

To the Pharisee, there are two categories of people: him, and everyone else. In the second group is a cadre of lawbreakers—the extortionists, impure, adulterers, and, of course, those rotten tax collectors. Fortunately for them, this gaggle of scoundrels is close enough to "eavesdrop on a man of his stratospheric piety."[3] As the Pharisee bellows on at close range, the tax collector breaks at a distance. Trembling in a fit of tears, he pleads for God's mercy and hopes that God will accept his discredited act of worship (vv. 9–14). He rips off the layers of religious pretense and bares his all to God.

Jesus asks the crowd a question to which they all know the answer: "Which one went home justified before God? Was it the Pharisee or the sinner?" It isn't the one who came to confess with his religious score card in hand, that's for sure. It's the poor in spirit. The one who has no résumé of pious achievement to offer. The shocking implication of the parable is that the sanctimonious and snarky Pharisee went home *unjustified*. His "self-rightness" repulsed God.

I learned this parable the hard way. Though I had read it many times, the Spirit had to teach it to me in the context of life.

CONFESSION WITH COMPARISON

I had an opportunity to take a driving class a couple of years ago. I was invited to be there by the kind officer who pulled me over for blowing through an "ambiguous" red light. I was irritated that I had to go to the four-hour driving class, but it was either the class or ruin my sterling driving record with a ticket. So I chose the class.

I showed up at the Post Falls, Idaho, Police Department at 6:00 p.m. I sat in the back. I observed that my fellow attendees were kind of a rough bunch. At the beginning of the class the instructor asked two questions: "Why are you here?" and "Do you deserve to be here?" I was the last to answer. At first I just sat there with arms folded, thinking to myself, "I don't need to be here with these *lawbreakers*. I'm not like *them*; I don't deserve *this*." My attitude worsened until something remarkable took place.

Every person in that class took ownership of their transgression. One by one, each one confessed their wrongdoing and admitted that they deserved to be there. This atmosphere of confession was like a battering ram to my intractable attitude. By the time they got to me, I was wrecked by God's Spirit. I confessed my offense and joined the fellowship of the Post Falls traffic violators. I learned that evening the meaning of Jesus's parable of the Pharisee and the tax collector. I discovered that self-righteousness is *confession with comparison*. It happens as we compare ourselves to all those other lawbreakers who are surely worse than us. It is an appeal to self-righteousness instead of God's righteousness. The Spirit comes to us and cuts through all that, bringing our sin into the light of the cross.

Remember that the "good" Pharisee in Jesus's story was at the temple to offer his sacrifice and pray. Triumphant. Polished. Impressed by all the wrong measurements. Like him, inwardly we know we're better than others. We know the Bible teaching at our church is superior. We are sure that our model of doing ministry is the most biblical one. We have so much to offer God compared to those other Christian "losers." We pray and we worship. But inwardly we are seething with spiritual snobbery.

You may be surprised to discover that it is not the Spirit's job to conform everyone to your likeness. It is the Spirit's job to transform disciples into Jesus's image.

A Universal Delusion

Probably the greatest misnomer about self-righteousness is that only religious people struggle with it. The truth: self-righteousness is the universal sin of humanity. Ask any person on the street or at the mall why they think God should give them eternal life, and they'll say something like, "I think I'm a pretty good person." This is the essence of self-righteousness. Both secular and sectarian groups alike are guilty of believing that they are good enough.

The Spirit of God reveals a barrier to our new life in Christ. It is the deception that we are well when we are really quite ill. It is the false belief that our conformity to some moral code keeps us in right standing, instead of the path of confession and humility.

Repentance is the natural response of a soul that is profoundly moved by the effort of God. To repent is to abandon any appeal to our own goodness and prudish virtue. It is an admission that we can no longer subsist on the broth and the slumgullion of a society gone mad with sin.

This is why we must bring our sin into the light and respond to the Spirit's conviction. It is impossible to see the beam of a flashlight on a sunlit beach. The full spectrum radiance of the cross washes out the flicker of our weak piety.

Confession is what I call a gateway discipline. It opens the door to all that is truly righteous. Humbly acknowledging our sin reminds us that our religious résumé is blank—we have no achievements, no saintly activity that will be acceptable to God at all. Only the Holy Spirit can make us righteous as we place our faith in Jesus alone.

You may think self-righteousness is only for buttoned-up Bible thumpers. Not true. Self-righteousness is the universal delusion that humanity has bought into. We believe that because we're not as bad as a serial killer or a sex trafficker, God will stamp us "OK" for eternity. But this is not the standard. Being good enough isn't good enough. Just "OK" isn't going to cut it.

The Spirit wants to drag my sin scratching and yowling into the light of the cross. Only by confronting the sin of a smug, self-righteous heart can I experience the Spirit's work of inner transformation. So how do we allow the Spirit to do His work of conviction? I'll end this chapter by giving you one, solid takeaway that will put you on the path to discovering the power of forgiveness.

CAN YOU HEAR THE SIRENS?

An article that appeared in Chuck Shepherd's *News of the Weird* recalls one of the worst robbery attempts of all time. As the story goes, two dim-witted thieves waited until a pawnshop closed, then drove their truck into the metal doors. The problem was that a steel grid protected the heavy doors. So the truck couldn't quite penetrate into the store. Luckily these geniuses brought plan B. Like a couple of urban lumberjacks, the thieves hopped out of the truck with chainsaws and went to work on what was left of the metal pawnshop doors and the iron grid.

The police arrived—sirens blaring and tires screeching. The criminals were easily apprehended because they never even noticed the officers behind them. They couldn't hear the police sirens over the earsplitting roar of their power tools chawing through twisted steel.

The role of the Spirit is to bring clarity to our state. But it is difficult to hear the sirens of God's Spirit when there is so much noise in our lives, the noise and the clatter produced by a bulging schedule and chain meetings. What we need is to get quiet— quiet enough to hear the Spirit's voice.

The barrier to a life of Spirit conviction is a self-right attitude. Thinking that we have nothing to confess. Believing the tired old lie that God will let you in His kingdom because you meet some minimal threshold of not being as bad as all those other rascals. The path to conviction is often solitude, tuning out the false voices of our culture and the racket of a busy world, and humbling yourself in the presence of a holy God who summons you by His Spirit—who means to arrest you and bring your sin into the light of His truth. If we will but confess our sins, He will be faithful and just to forgive us and wash us clean of a heart sullied by self-righteousness (1 John 1:9).

The question is, *Can you hear the Spirit's sirens?*

6

THE NEW AND IMPROVED YOU

The Spirit renovates our hearts.

> The greatest need you and I have—the
> greatest need of collective humanity—
> is renovation of our heart.[1]
> —DALLAS WILLARD—
> *Renovation of the Heart*

WESTERN CULTURE IS increasingly obsessed with avoiding death. We want to stay around as long as we can and hopefully look good doing it. It's natural to want to prolong your life. Who wouldn't want a little more time with children, spouses, or parents? The late Steve Jobs said it best: "Even people who want to go to heaven don't want to die to get there."[2] Clinging to life is a natural instinct. What isn't so natural is the weird and downright morbid fascination that many have with staying young, or at least, looking young.

In her revealing book *Beauty Junkies*, *New York Times* author Alex Kuczynski documented the secretive world of our beauty-obsessed culture. She describes a fat-injecting procedure by "Dr. Pat," a well-known dermatologist in New York. The procedure involved extracting the fat from her friend's buttocks and then injecting it into the woman's face:

> I watched Dr. Pat bring out one of the vials of fat and, using a fine subcutaneous needle, inject the contents of one of the syringes into the woman's cheeks and

nasolabial folds—the lines that run from the nose to the mouth. The fat was surprisingly thick and bright yellow, a neon sludge that looks almost exactly like the lemon-flavored cake frosting you might buy in a plastic Betty Crocker tub at the supermarket. Just greasier. The procedure is called autologous fat transfer—that is, moving fat from one part of the body to another.[3]

Though I was aware that people were getting surgical enhancements to slow the effects of aging, I was unaware and, I have to say, aghast at the grotesque and grisly procedures described in Kuczynski's book. Everything from shortening toes so that customers can fit into designer shoes, to extracting collagen from cadavers and harvesting fetal foreskin cells for therapy.

Yikes! All for the sake of recapturing the allure of youth and counteracting the dreadful effects of gravity, time, and stress. I put Kuczynski's book down and thought, "How is it that we have come to such a vulgar and superficial obsession with youth?"

I had sent the question out into the universe, thinking that I would discover the answer through hours of meditating on the Psalms or something. But I didn't have to wait long for the solution. The cosmos instantly responded...

"We're idolaters who crave shortcuts."

We worship at the altar of physical beauty and have little patience for the hard-fought victories of character growth or health. I live in an unprecedented age where if I don't like the length of my nose, I can see a surgeon for some facial "sculpting."

If I don't want to bother with a gym membership to deal with that muffin top figure I've developed through years of poor diet and lack of exercise, I can just lipo the fat out.

If I don't like my chalky and puckish complexion, I can nuke my skin at the local tanning coffins.

And if I no longer care for those annoying wrinkles above my lip, I can punch up and rejuvenate my skin by injecting some botulism or butt fat into my face.

We may be able to temporarily change our appearance like a tailor altering a suit, but eventually whatever we lift is going to sag again. Medical miracles ultimately fail. As my friend Brian likes to say, "Even Lazarus eventually died again." Before long, those weird and unnatural collagen injections will wear off. Gravity and time have a way of relentlessly stalking us.

OLDER BUT NEWER

Paul told the Corinthians, "Therefore we do not lose heart. Though outwardly we are wasting away, yet inwardly we are being renewed day by day. For our light and momentary troubles are achieving for us an eternal glory that far outweighs them all" (2 Cor. 4:16–17). If I'm reading this passage correctly, then as we believers get older, we are actually getting newer.

The year my little boy Tyler was born is the same year we lost my wife's grandpa Johnny. Grandpa Johnny was the kindest old gentleman you would ever know this side of eternity. It struck me that as we were saying hello to a brand-new life entering the world, we were saying good-bye to a life well lived—an old life on his way into God's presence for eternity.

Someone's always coming and going, aren't they? This reminded me that someday this brand-new little baby with perfectly soft skin and big brown eyes—experiencing the world for the first time—this same boy will someday be an old man. And he'll be going and his great-grandkids will be just arriving. This is the pattern of life. You live—you die.

You can't change that.

Though we should take care of our bodies with good diet and exercise, we should also acknowledge that we have a shelf life. This is why our focus must be on spiritual transformation and future resurrection. Jesus told an educated rabbi in His day that unless he was born anew by the Spirit, he would never enter the kingdom of God. (See John 3:5–8.) The studious, thought-burdened rabbi couldn't understand. He complained that it was impossible for him to reenter his mother's womb and be born again.

Jesus scolded him for his overly literal interpretation: "So let Me get this straight. You are Israel's educator about heavenly things, and yet you don't even understand the most rudimentary fact concerning participation in the kingdom?" Rabbi Jesus continued the lesson, "It's like this, Nick. People give birth to people all the time. But only the Spirit can give birth to a new spirit. This new birth is the entry point into the kingdom of God." (See John 3.)

In the last chapter we learned that the Spirit starts with conviction of sin. Then the Spirit begins the process of our inner renovation the moment we come to Jesus in faith. Though we are reborn instantly and become new creations the moment we enter the kingdom, spiritual transformation of our inner man isn't automatic. If it were, then we wouldn't have any New Testament letters from Paul to the early church.

What if we obsessed over our inner transformation by the Spirit as much as we worried about the length of our noses, the whiteness of our teeth, and the wrinkles on our brows? What if in addition to our preoccupation with our physical lives, we focused on being transformed into the character and likeness of Jesus? The key to this spiritual renovation is obedience from the heart.

OBEDIENCE ON THE RUN

Police Chief Michael Hutter attempted to pull over Nita Friedman for erratic and reckless driving. This happened on US Highway 95, in Bonner's Ferry, a town just north of where I live in Idaho.

Hutter flipped on his lights and let out a *squawk* from his siren. But instead of pulling over to the side of the road, the sixty-six-year-old Mrs. Friedman took a hard left and just kept going. The chief called it in, and the police chased the woman for fifteen miles through two counties. Finally they put out a spike strip in front of her car and blew out her tires.

Amazingly during the fifteen-mile chase, Friedman never once exceeded the speed limit. In fact, several times during the chase she yielded to oncoming traffic and politely used her signal lights, slowly making left and right turns. She was charged with reckless driving while following the speed limit and obeying other minor traffic laws. This was clearly a case of trivial obedience on the run.[4]

As pastors, we sit with people on many occasions listening to bad decisions made in the name of God. The conversations usually go something like this: "I had a disagreement with my employer regarding their management style, and so I feel the Lord leading me to find another job." Or how about this one: "Yeah, my wife and I are having trouble, and so I've prayed about it and feel like God is calling me to get out of the marriage and find a new spouse." Here's my favorite one: "I just don't feel comfortable in this church. Too many demands on my time and money. And someone in my small group disagreed with me, and so I think God is speaking to me to find another church, Pastor Jeff." In most of these cases the person is choosing to bail on a hard situation and then pinning their bad decisions or lack of commitment on God.

But they prayed about it. They even found a passage in the Book of Joshua encouraging them to "move on" and "take new territory" or some off-the-wall, out-of-context scripture that has nothing to do with their poor decisions. This kind of decision making is nothing more than trivial obedience while our heart is hauling away from God.

Paul referred to this kind of disjointed behavior as "having a form of godliness but denying its power" (2 Tim. 3:5). Paul was referring to the windy piety and the nebulous abstractions of pagan religion.[5] We practice empty religion every time we spiritualize our rebellion. It is obedience to minor externalities while inwardly we are headed in the opposite direction from God's heart. It's phony spirituality. The net effect of this false spirituality is spiritual incompetence. This kind of trifling conformity on the religious margins stops just short of true inner change. Nothing is more damaging to our progress than the leaky theology of changeless religion. But the good news is that with the Spirit's help, we can choose to change. We can turn it around. We can pull over before we hit the spike strips and wreck our marriages, our relationships, and our character.

Spirit Competence

There is perhaps no better example of a turnaround church than the congregation in Corinth. We noted earlier that Paul wrote them a letter to correct their character problems. Yet in Paul's follow-up letter to them, it may surprise you to learn that they had taken his advice to heart. "You yourselves are our letter," Paul declared, "written on our hearts, known and read by everybody. You show that you are a letter from Christ, the result of our ministry, written not with ink but with the Spirit of the living God, not on tablets of stone but on tablets of human hearts" (2 Cor. 3:2–3). What a turnaround story. In his first letter to the Corinthians Paul called them "spiritual nurslings." Now, in this follow-up correspondence, Paul calls them living epistles written by the same Spirit who inspired the Bible!

Paul shows us that the end game in our transformation is mastering the text in life. The living Word of God was incarnated in Jesus, and the believer must learn to apply the Word in the power of the Spirit. The Corinthians' response to Paul's previous letter resulted in their embodying the principles of the Word of Life and becoming, in a sense, the *word in life.*

Paul goes on to speak of the Spirit competence they displayed in the Corinthians' midst. "Not that we are competent in ourselves to claim anything for ourselves, but our competence comes from God. He has made us competent as ministers of a new covenant—not of the letter but of the Spirit; for the letter kills, but the Spirit gives life" (2 Cor. 3:5–6). Paul draws our attention to a different kind of proficiency—it is Spirit competence. Do you ever sit in church and think, "Man, I hope my pastor has Spirit competence this morning"? But Paul says that a minister of the gospel needs spiritual proficiency in the new covenant. That's why he described himself to them as "an expert builder" (1 Cor. 3:10). Eldon Trueblood once stated, "Holy shoddy is still shoddy."[6] Just because you're a Christian or a minister of the gospel doesn't mean you know what you're doing.

Transformed living begins with Spirit competence. It happens as we seek to obey the Word in the power of the Spirit. The Spirit meets us at the intersection of our obedience and faith. As we grow in our skill with God's Word, living out its principles in life, we are inwardly transformed. The interior transformation is exteriorized into our actions.

BY FITS AND STARTS

Paul concluded, "Now the Lord is the Spirit, and where the Spirit of the Lord is, there is freedom. And we, who with unveiled faces all reflect the Lord's glory, are being transformed into his likeness with ever-increasing glory, which comes from the Lord, who is the Spirit" (2 Cor. 3:17–18).

Have you ever restored anything to its original condition? My father-in-law is restoring an old 1940s truck and making sure that it looks just like the original. Well, pretty close to the original, anyway. No fancy stuff—he wants it to be the way it was in the old days. Funny thing is, he's been restoring it over a period of many years—piece by piece, bit by bit, restoring it to its former glory. And every shiny, new, restored part is one more piece of its former glory.

Paul stated that as we reflect on the Lord's glory by the Spirit, we are being transformed into Jesus's image incrementally. Step by step, by fits and starts, we are restored into His image. We are remade, believing that the Spirit will meet us at the point of our faithfulness, converting us into the image of His glorious Son.

In the process He doesn't strip us of our personalities, making us featureless drones bereft of personhood or individuality. On the contrary, there is a direct correspondence to our old selves. But we are refit, remade for kingdom life. You still have the same idiosyncratic quirks and personality tics you've always had. It's still you, just the new-and-improved version. And the new you starts with a new heart. It continues in the process of daily transformation through obedience to the Spirit and God's truth.

In the following chapters we'll explore more specifically how the Lord transforms us bit by bit and glory by glory. The Spirit enables us to meet our obligations, and He does this as we learn Jesus's teachings in the context of life.

7

WHEN I SAY "JUMP!"

The Spirit empowers us to meet our obligations.

Without God's Spirit, there is nothing we can do
that will count for God's kingdom. Without God's
Spirit, the church simply can't be the church.[1]
—N. T. WRIGHT—
Simply Christian

WHEN MY BOYS were little, they loved to put on their
Incredible Hulk feet slippers and green jammies and play
a game we called "Hulk Jump." My little boy Logan in particular
loved this game. I would stand behind him, grab him under the
arms, and say, "OK, get ready. When Daddy says jump, you jump
with all you've got, all right?" He would nod, bend his knees, and
it was T-minus five to launch.

T-minus five...four...three...

As soon as I'd say, "Jump!" the boy would launch with all his
might. I'd lift him all the way up to the ceiling. By the time little
Logan made it to his bed, he was exhausted from bouncing and
pinging and growling all over the house. But he had jumped
higher, longer, and farther than he could have ever imagined in
his own strength.

This is a picture of how the Spirit empowers us. He inhabits
our efforts. He energizes our activity and comes alongside our
initiatives.

When you jump, He lifts.

Now, He doesn't approve of everything we do. And He doesn't automatically endorse all of our activity on His behalf. I suspect there is an awful lot of Spirit-less wheel spinning in the church today. I also suspect that the Spirit is doing a lot more than we may be aware of.

The Fantasy of the Uninitiated

Wouldn't it be great if the Christian life were easy? That's not to say that believers don't have an easier go at the challenges that are common to humanity. This notion of "easier" is revealed in Old Testament poetic language as "making your crooked paths straight." There were few things in the ancient world more stressful than traveling around sinuous paths and steep valleys where brigands might hide around the next turn to assault you. Ancient Palestine was known for these twisted and dusty trails. So the picture of giving a traveler a "straight" and level path was a nice sentiment. And it's sometimes true of the Christian life.

But, more often than not, the Christian life is hard work. Tough challenges are the lot of all believers. The truth is that sometimes we pray, we worship, we work hard, and we trust that the Spirit will show up and change lives. But often, building the kingdom involves some sweat equity. We pour our lives into others as we believe in faith that the Spirit will work powerfully. This has been the pattern since God unveiled His agenda of giving us the Spirit.

For example, I'm sure John the Baptist expected Jesus to get him out of jail. So he sent a disciple to ask, "Are You the One? Or should we look for another?"

What kind of question was that?

How could John, the last prophet of the Old Testament—the one who saw the Spirit descend on Jesus and heard the voice from heaven—how could he have asked such a question? Easy. This is the sort of question that is born out of desperation. The question embedded within the question was, "And if You are the

One, when are You going to bring the smack down on Herod and get me out of this prison cell?" But the answer was not what John the Baptist had hoped. Yes, Jesus was the Messiah, but John's situation in prison would get worse, not better. Jesus even cited all the miracles He was doing *for everyone else* as evidence that He was the Christ. I'm sure John must have thought, "Oh. How comforting."

Likewise it was hard for the apostle James to learn that the prayers of the house church in Jerusalem hadn't worked. The same people praying for him were praying for Peter to be released. Unlike Peter, who was delivered from jail by an angelic messenger, James would be martyred for Christ. That was hard.

It was also hard for Paul to lose his rabbinic pedigree and find himself being chased from town to town and beaten and left for dead, hungry on occasion, terrified by gale force winds threatening to wreck his ship, and doing the occasional stint in a city dungeon. *That* was hard.

So anyone who imagines that the Christian life is just an endless chain of delightful experiences lived out on the corner of easy street just doesn't get it. To borrow Anne Lamott's words, this is just "the fantasy of the uninitiated."[2] Life is hard. And the Christian life can be difficult at times. But God has sent us the Spirit that we may be empowered beyond our abilities. We have assistance for life's challenges that our unbelieving neighbors do not have. But how do we get on the fast track to this power?

In this chapter we'll establish that the power of the Spirit comes to a surrendered heart that is faithfully engaged in Christian community and fellowship. The Spirit empowers us to meet our obligations as believers.

"Is This a Peaceful Visit, Seer?"

One of the most compelling stories of God's Spirit making a difference is the life of David. David's story surfaces one indispensable principle of Spirit empowerment.

David, the son of Jesse, was, in effect, rejected seven times before he was anointed king. In fact, David's chances were so slim that it didn't even occur to Jesse to have him present for the royal tryouts with the prophet Samuel (1 Sam. 16:1–13). Without a doubt this was a monumental decision. Only the finest specimens need apply for the position of Israel's next king.

When Samuel arrived in Bethlehem, the city elders came trembling to meet him and asked, "Is this a peaceful visit, seer?" (See 1 Samuel 16:4.) I take it by the elders' ominous question that the prophet was not known for social visits.

Bethlehem's elders were justified in their concern about Samuel's intentions. The word on the street concerning the prophet was that he had a zero tolerance policy for disobedience. King Saul, for example, had been instructed by God to wipe out all of the wicked and barbaric Amalekites. Yet, for whatever reason, Saul spared Agag, the Amalekite king. When Samuel found out about this, he had Agag brought before the royal court, and the prophet killed him on the spot (1 Sam. 15:33).

An Irresistible Quality

So Bethlehem's elders likely concluded that when the prophet shows up to your town, one of two things is going to happen: you are either going to be the host site for a holy sacrifice to God, or your village sign is going to read, "The town formerly known as…"

Turns out that Samuel isn't there to slay the Bethlehemites for being in violation of Torah protocol. On the contrary, Samuel's official business is to worship Yahweh in Bethlehem. Unofficially he is on a clandestine mission to discover and anoint the next king of Israel.

At God's direction the prophet focuses his attention on a particular family in Bethlehem—the house of Jesse. One by one the sons of Jesse strut their stuff. And one by one, at the direction of the Lord, the mystic seer rejects them—*all of them.*

"Do you have any more sons, Jesse?" Samuel asks.

"Well, yes. There's that other one. But he's pasturing the flock right now."

"Well, send someone out to fetch him at once."

A messenger runs out to retrieve the young shepherd. David drops his staff and bolts into the village, leaving a narrow trail of dust in his wake. God has a special place in His heart for all those *other ones* out there in the field of obscurity.

Though Samuel isn't supposed to size up the candidates based on outward criteria, the prophet just can't help himself. Scripture's assessment of David's appearance basically reads, "Not bad." David's bourbon-colored eyes sparkle. Though he lacks the brawn and mass of his older brothers, he appears to be in fine pastoral form—lithe and lean and possessing a handsome face with sharp angles. He is neither a rippling wall of strength, nor is he the undernourished weakling of Hollywood depictions. He is somewhere in between. David is both artist and lion killer. His belt is outfitted with a leather sling and a hide pouch for stones, the humble armaments of a shepherd. In him is the seed of greatness.

Whatever physical deficiencies he may have had, he possesses an irresistible quality to God—*his heart is fully surrendered.* God's way of putting it was, "He is a man who pursues My very heart."

David is dead last, and he knows it. Before Samuel can begin the interview, God whispers into the prophet's inner ear, "That's him. He's the one. Anoint him." Then the prophet empties his horn of oil on David's head, the Spirit seizes the young man, and the nation of Israel will never be the same.

God is still trolling the margins, looking for people who love Him deeply from the heart, people who will abandon the virulent strain of idolatry and self-worship that permeate our society.

God wants fully devoted followers and worshippers. To God, these rejects are irresistible.

David was a nobody from nowhere. He knew exactly what it was like to be dead last on a list of very important "somebodies."

Some things just can't be measured. Some things only God Himself can see. What made the difference in his life was a surrendered heart and the Spirit's anointing.

The first secret to the power of the Spirit is that we must relinquish the control of our lives to the Father. God anoints the heart of one who is fully submitted and surrendered to His will. It takes hard work to live in submission to God. But God always meets the submitted man or woman with a supernatural commitment. The difference between David's day and ours is that God's Spirit has now been poured out on all flesh, and every believer can know the "stamp of eternity."[3] It is God's anointing, His supernatural endorsement on a surrendered life.

But if God's power were just a matter of personal devotion and surrender, then there would be no need for community. The promise of the Spirit and power is for everyone who would believe and surrender (Acts 2:42). This anointing is now a community affair. God has sent His Spirit to empower the submitted individual and to amplify that power in the context of Christian community.

INTO THE FRAY

Every man has his limits.

I was fourteen years old, and my dad had enough. Dad was only a seasonal churchgoer. He showed up for Christmas, Easter, and the occasional baptism, but he didn't have much use for church otherwise.

Dad was a large, violent storm of a man, whose muscular arms were annotated with tattoos and welding scars. But underneath all that gruff lay a soft spot for troubled kids—probably because he had been one himself, dropping out of high school, living on the street when he was sixteen, and supporting himself by learning a trade. For several years he had tried to rehabilitate a couple of young men who regularly broke into our home and robbed us while we were away on vacation or out of town. But his kindness was answered with contempt. And the one thing my father had little patience for was contemptuous behavior.

The convenience store next door was an untidy old hovel with smooth wooden floors, a creaky door, and no air-conditioning. I regularly hung out at the old store and would finish off a soda before heading home. The two young thieves lived in the house right next to that old store. Before I had a chance to head toward home, my dad drove by and stopped to pick me up. I hopped in the passenger's seat, and Dad put the car in gear and started to drive away.

The two young thieves came out of the little house and flipped Dad a choice finger and called him a name I can't repeat in a Christian book.

He slammed on the brakes and came out of that car like a racer responding to a starter pistol. The first young man stepped up, and just like that, Dad broke his nose. Before the other one had a chance to say, "Who do you think you are, old ma—" *Crack!* He got the left hand.

I shouted, "All riggght!" and jumped out of the car. I don't remember much of the fight; I just remember jumping into the fray and landing right in the middle of all of it—right alongside my dad. And it was ridiculous! I thought I was hot stuff back then, but in retrospect it was like some silly scene out of *The Dukes of Hazzard* (cue the banjo chase music).

At some point we all had enough, and so we parted company with bumps and bruises and fat lips. We got back in the car, and my dad got kind of choked up. He put the cigarette to his lips that he'd left glowing in the ashtray and said with a jittery grin, "Hey, boy. I'm glad you did that."

"Did what, Daddy?"

"I'm glad you got out of the car. Thanks for getting in there with your old man." And he never mentioned it again. I learned in that weird dysfunctional moment the meaning and power of loyalty.

Loyalty is such an uncomplicated quality, isn't it? Loyalty is the subatomic stuff of tight, close relationships. And close Christian relationships are the catalyst for unleashing the Spirit's power in our world today. The Spirit empowers us through personal surrender and devotion to God, and He amplifies that power as we engage in faithful, loyal Christian community. This is what enables us to be His worshippers and His witnesses.

TOE TO TOE, SHOULDER TO SHOULDER

As I read the book of Philippians, I think the apostle Paul is having a similar moment with the Philippian church that my dad had with me. Sitting in a Roman jail, feeling like he's the only one contending for this gospel, he fights for its very existence while false teachers spread horrible rumors about him. In the midst of all this he receives an unbelievable gift of support from these Philippian Christians. In Rome, when you got put in jail, you didn't get three squares a day, cable TV, and a weight room. If you didn't have family or friends who could support you, then you died in jail.[4] The Philippians were the only church who sent Paul supplies. Those provisions kept him alive.

Paul's letter to them was a joyful thank-you note. Paul wrote it to say, "Thank you for jumping into the fray with me. Thank you for contending by my side and for getting in there with your old apostle." Paul tells them to fight the good fight together:

> Only conduct yourselves in a manner worthy of the gospel of Christ so that—whether I come and see you or whether I remain absent—I should hear that you are standing firm in one spirit, with one mind, by contending side by side for the faith of the gospel, and by not being intimidated in any way by your opponents.
> —PHILIPPIANS 1:27–28, NET

Paul wanted to thank these Philippian Christians for partnering and contending for this gospel in spite of the fanatical harassment of their pagan peers.

The Philippian Christians had stayed true, and Paul could hardly contain his joy. In fact, he uses the word *joy* in this short letter more than in his other letters combined. Then he prays that they would complete his joy by being unified in love and being one in spirit (Phil. 2:2). This is the essence of our power. It is a Spirit bond that is strengthened as we go toe to toe with the enemies of the gospel, standing shoulder to shoulder with each other.

Have you ever had someone who was this loyal to you? I mean an all-in, taking-a-bullet-for-you kind of friend? Strong, unbreakable Christian union is a crucial factor to unleashing the Spirit's power in our midst. Here's how Jesus put it: "I in them and you in me. May they be brought to complete unity to let the world know that you sent me and have loved them even as you have loved me" (John 17:23). The greater the unity, the greater our Christian witness to the world. Our influence on the community is exactly proportional to our capacity for unity.

The power of God was unleashed at Pentecost as "they were all together in one place" (Acts 2:1). They were together with arms locked, prepared to live and die *together*. It doesn't just mean that they were together in the same room. They were one in spirit with a single devotion and a single mind. That kind of bond gets forged in the crucible of persecution, not in the comfort of a mall. It gets forged when a company of soldiers hunkers side by side in the trenches with bullets zipping past their heads, fighting a common enemy and standing for a common cause.

You can encounter God's Spirit powerfully in personal devotion and surrender. But community can intensify that encounter and strengthen your commitment. N. T. Wright asks, "What would it mean for your church fellowship to live as a colony of heaven with the responsibility to bring the life and rule of heaven to bear on earth?"[5] The Spirit comes powerfully through Christian fellowship, strengthened by the bonds of loyalty. This is how we bring heaven's power and rule into our world.

Paul told the Philippians, "I want to know Christ and the power of his resurrection and the fellowship of sharing in his sufferings, becoming like him in his death" (Phil. 3:10). Curious verse. The phrase "fellowship of sharing in his sufferings" is a community designation. The "fellowship" in Paul's letters always refers to a voluntary association of people—together—experiencing the mystical union of the Spirit. We participate in Christ's death and resurrection. We are the fellowship of the suffering who anticipate future resurrection by the Spirit's power. The power of the resurrection is in the fellowship. Paul continues:

> But our citizenship is in heaven. And we eagerly await a Savior from there, the Lord Jesus Christ, who, by the power that enables him to bring everything under his control, will transform our lowly bodies so that they will be like his glorious body.
>
> —Philippians 3:20–21

The power of the Holy Spirit is available to the redeemed sons and daughters of God who, like David, have surrendered their hearts and who, like the Philippians, are linked into a loyal Spirit community.

But we should not fantasize that this is an easy vocation. Passion and unity are hard won. It is difficult work to create a church environment where people pursue God's very heart and where they stand together in loyalty. These are, in fact, the two areas where Satan is most at work. If he can make a church inert and lazy—if he can blunt the edge of our passion—then he'll succeed at turning us into powerless church attenders. Then all he has to do is get people quibbling over stupid stuff. If he can slake our thirst for God and splinter us into factions, then he'll have free rein in the church. We'll be hobbled and unable to impact our community or the world. We'll be "that church" in the neighborhood where an outsider would never dare to stumble.

But the church that loves God passionately and is devoted to others selflessly will get God's attention. These are irresistible qualities to God. God manifests His power in such a transformational environment.

UNTIL YOU RECEIVE POWER

God's presence is the power we need to live up to our obligations as worshippers and witnesses. The apostles were to wait in Jerusalem until they had received the Spirit (Acts 1:4). Jesus told the disciples that they would receive power when the Spirit came upon them—not power to witness, but power to *be His witnesses* (v. 8). After they had received the Spirit, they got busy working, worshipping, and serving in His power.

Until we have received the Spirit, the best we'll ever be able to do is to become accomplished at empty religion. For the church that passionately loves God and selflessly loves and serves one another, God will always one-up us.

We can't outgive Him.

We can't outwork Him.

We can't outlove Him or out-suffer Him.

You cannot outdo God in anything. When you jump, He lifts. When you give, He multiplies. When you share your life and your story, He anoints—powerfully, mysteriously, and unflinchingly. Until we are clothed in this power, we have nothing but potential. The minute we are empowered by the Spirit, that potential becomes actual. We are able to do what He's summoned us to do, and we are able to become the people He wants us to become—loving God and loving others (more about that in a later chapter). His power is what enables us to march out into our world and proclaim the countercultural truth—Jesus has won the victory, and God is the King of the world.

8

UNLIMITED BANDWIDTH

The Spirit gives life through the Word.

> The Holy Spirit may be distinguished from the
> Word, but to separate the Word and the Spirit is
> spiritually fatal. The Holy Spirit teaches, leads,
> and speaks to us through the Word and with the
> Word, not apart from or against the Word.[1]
> —R. C. SPROUL—
> *The Mystery of the Holy Spirit*

THE STORY IS told of an elderly woman who came home from church after studying the Book of Acts and found a thief ripping her off. The intruder didn't hear the lady come in, and standing behind him, she blurted out the first thing that came to mind. It was the scripture from the morning's lesson.

"Acts 2:38!" she shouted. The scripture reads, "Each of you must repent of your sins and turn to God, and be baptized in the name of Jesus Christ" (Acts 2:38, NLT).

The thief was startled and froze as if he'd been splashed with liquid nitrogen. The lady called 911, and the man didn't move a muscle until the police got there. It was a miracle, or so it seemed. The officers cuffed the intruder and put him in the police car.

The woman explained to the officer that she just quoted a Bible verse—Acts 2:38, and the man was miraculously unable to move.

But the arresting officer wasn't buying it. Before driving off to the police station, he turned and asked the thief, "Man, I gotta know. That little old lady couldn't have stopped you if she wanted to. Why did you freeze when she quoted the Bible verse at you?"

"Bible verse?" the thief said in shock. "I didn't hear no Bible verse—that woman told me she had an ax and two 38s, and that's why I froze."

Paul stated that the Scriptures have the power to stop us cold, to convict us of sin, to confront our false beliefs, and to transform us into the likeness of Jesus. Scripture has this power because the Holy Spirit has inspired it and because the Spirit is the active agent in teaching us Jesus's truth. In this chapter we'll explore the power of Jesus's statement, "The words I have spoken to you are spirit and they are life" (John 6:63). It is God's Spirit who flips the switch and enlightens us to His revealed Word.

A "SAFE" CREEDAL STATEMENT

Over the years the Scriptures have become the object of ridicule and the focus of some very fine Christian apologetics. The Greek word *apologeo* means "to offer a defense." Historically we've become adept at defending the gospel against the haters.

Very early on the church was forced to defend against false doctrine and false Christianities—heretical movements that sought to irrevocably alter the foundation of the Christian faith. Defending against false doctrine over the centuries has honed our ability to protect the sacred. This started at least as far back as Paul defending the gospel in the synagogues and to the Romans (Gal. 2:14; Col. 1:19–20). Additionally Paul often had to distinguish the Christian faith from the cultic enterprise of the Greco-Roman world. Christianity faced a lot of peer pressure to blend and fit in with local pagan religions. As the gospel went out to inhabit the culture, it was always in danger of being contaminated by false belief systems.

Right after the apostolic era (AD 100) men like Justin the Martyr and Tatian undertook a defense of the faith.[2] As groups like the Marcionites and Montanists tried to modify God's Word, the church had to officially canonize, or collect, the writings of the apostles. We've been vigilant in protecting the sacred text ever since. And rightly so. Paul commanded Timothy to watch his life and doctrine closely (1 Tim. 4:16). We are instructed to defend our hope, answering any and all objections to our faith (1 Pet. 3:15).

Yet too much of an emphasis on safeguarding the past can lead to an undue reverence of it. We begin to view it as our job to narrow the frequency band by which God can speak and be spoken to. "Protect the sacred trust at all costs" becomes our mantra. Yet our tendency has been to sacrifice being led by the Spirit in favor of a safe creedal statement. But this clearly is a false choice. We can have both. Because God operates at a larger bandwidth than we do, we need to be open to encountering Him in ways that are both biblically informed and out of our comfort zone.

CHRISTIAN DEISM

Growing up, I was repeatedly told in church and youth camps, "Now that we have a Bible, we have no need for miracles or for God to speak to us today." But what if God wants to speak to me today about something specific? "Go read your Bible" was always the answer. Dallas Willard addressed this:

> Today something that could be called "Bible deism" is prevalent, particularly in conservative religious circles. Classical deism, associated with the extreme rationalism of the sixteenth to eighteenth centuries, held that God created his world complete and perfect and then went away, leaving humanity to its own devices. God no longer offered individualized intervention in the lives of human beings, no miracles. Bible deism similarly holds that God gave us the Bible and then went away, leaving us to make what we could of it, with no individual communication either through the Bible or otherwise.[3]

I suspect that the reason why some have replaced a dynamic and Spirit-filled faith with "Bible deism" is that Bible deism is safer than the kind of Christianity we see in the New Testament. New Testament Christianity is strange and foreign to us because we live in a culture dominated by philosophical naturalism. Philosophical naturalism is the notion that only the material world exists. The naturalist believes that all of the "stuff" in the universe owes its existence and emergence to the natural world.[4] The naturalist cannot accept a spiritual, supernatural, or metaphysical category of existence.

Now, science has much to offer us. Science can be a helpful way to look at our world. But the unscientific belief that only the natural world exists is incompatible with our Christian commitment. And no Christian would say that they are a naturalist or a Bible deist. Yet, while many of us say we believe in a supernatural God, we live as if this supernatural God has wound up the universe, left it spinning, and fled the scene.

I recently had this discussion with a hard-core cessationist friend of mine. Extreme cessasionism maintains that all supernatural occurrences are relegated to biblical days and don't occur beyond the first century—particularly what they call the "sign gifts." I said to him, "You know, if you and I were in the same room with atheists like Richard Dawkins or Sam Harris, we would team up and vigorously defend the existence of a supernatural God to them. Then, as soon as the atheists left the room, we'd haggle over whether this supernatural God actually *does* supernatural things."

He said, "I think you might be on to something there."

We're reluctant to listen to the supernatural voice of God because that sort of thing doesn't fit into any of our sensory categories. It makes us uncomfortable. I submit that we have allowed more of the naturalist worldview to seep into our Christian belief system than we would care to admit. Like philosophical and secular naturalism, Christian naturalism is allergic to anything that cannot be explained by the senses.

When God doesn't fit into our neat little taxonomies, we are then tempted to *make Him fit*. In doing so, we inadvertently squeeze Him into a "God Box."

Burn Your Box

As I look at the church today, I see lots of little boxes that we've constructed for God to live in. The Spirit doesn't just want to break out of these boxes; He wants to incinerate them.

Some people put Him in the "First-Century Box."

This box consigns God's power and voice to the first century. Somehow the sovereign God of Scripture mysteriously lost His sovereignty at the close of the apostolic age. This is surely a safe box for God to be in—and safe for us, as well. We don't have to worry about all that strange supernatural stuff in the Bible.

Some of us have stuffed God into the "Therapeutic Deity Box."

This box reduces God to nothing more than a celestial therapist who exists to comfort us when things go wrong. This box has no room for discipleship training because it's "too hard." The people who use this therapeutic deity box only relate to God when He is handing out fish and loaves, but they have little appetite for His "flesh" or His "blood" (John 6:1–14, 25–59). That is, they call on God when the shelves are bare and the pantry is low, but they aren't interested in the mysterious and intimate communion with Jesus through His broken body and shed blood. When these folks discover that Christianity will cost them, they quickly bail in search of a "Christianity" that only *coddles* them.

Still others put him in the "Heavenly Vending Machine Box."

This box looks at God like a set of codes that need to be broken. Once we can punch up the right prophetic cryptogram or the right combination of blessing "codes," we should be able to get what we want from God. We hit A-7, and out pops our magical blessing. Whenever God is reduced to a code that needs to be cracked or a complicated encryption program that needs to be hacked in order to get a blessing, then we've fabricated a Jesus that doesn't exist.

And some have constructed a "Bible Box."

We are told that we will find God safely tucked away in the compartments of Scripture—that discovering Him happens as we dissect the text like a frog on a biology lab table. The Bible becomes the object of our study instead of the manual for living. To be sure, we should study Scripture and we should do our homework, but to reduce our interactions with God to *mere* exegesis of text is like walking the Emmaus Road, listening to the hidden Jesus speak, and then experiencing no burning of heart— no fire in our chest for more of Him. The burning heart invites Jesus in for intimate communion (Luke 24). It always wants more than mere instruction.

If we think for one second that God will be sequestered in any shrine or monument or reductionist box that we build for Him, we've got another "think" coming. The incarnate Word of God wants to inhabit every square inch of our existence. He wants to show us that the kingdom of heaven is not far off—safely tucked away in the first century somewhere; the kingdom of heaven is *near*. He was incarnate in a man, His teachings captured in a sacred text, and now He wants to inhabit every microcosm of your existence—speaking to you by the Spirit from out of your context.

God's Word, Incarnate in Jesus

Jesus was the incarnate, or personified Word of God. Jesus stated, "The Spirit gives life.... The words I have spoken to you are spirit and they are life" (John 6:63). The Spirit's life comes through the Word. John asserted, "In the beginning was the Word, and the Word was with God, and the Word was God" (John 1:1). Speaking of Jesus's incarnation, John wrote, "The Word became flesh and made his dwelling among us" (v. 14). Jesus's words were spirit and life. Wherever God speaks, God is. And God was speaking in Jesus, not as an Old Testament representative of God, but as God's authentic voice in the flesh.

The author of Hebrews also echoed this when he stated, "The Son is the radiance of God's glory and the exact representation of his being, sustaining all things by his powerful word" (Heb. 1:3).

Jesus assumed a scandalous authority to speak as God. When Jesus made the statement, "You have heard it said...but I say to you...," He knew that this sort of saying was forbidden in His Jewish culture. The rabbis always cited legal precedent in their *Halakah*, or binding legal rulings on Torah.[5] The rabbi would have to quote from either an authority in the school of *Shammai* or a recognized authority in the school of *Hillel*. Shammai and Hillel were the last two authoritative leaders of the *Zugoth*, which means "pair" of authoritative teachers.[6] Jesus cites from neither school, but instead He claims to be the final authority. Rabbinic historian Jacob Neusner remarked:

> Yes, I would have been astonished. Here is a Torah-teacher who says in his own name what the Torah says in God's name. It is one thing to say on one's own how a basic teaching of the Torah shapes the everyday....It is quite another to say that the Torah says one thing, but I say...then to announce in one's own name what God set forth at Sinai....I am troubled not so much by the message, though I might take exception to this or that, as I am by the messenger. The reason is that, in form these statements are jarring. Standing on the mountain, Jesus' use of language, "You have heard that it was said...but I say to you" contrasts strikingly with Moses' language at Mount Sinai. Jesus speaks, not as a sage nor as a prophet.[7]

Neusner is echoing a common difficulty among rabbinic Jews with Jesus's statement in the Sermon on the Mount. Jesus presumes to speak *as* God, not to just relay a message *from* God. It was considered more than "bad form." It was anathema. No one stands in the place of God and amends God's Word in his own name.

Blasphemy! Heresy!

No wonder they cried foul so often when Jesus taught and spoke to His followers. These are the kinds of things that Jesus was doing all over the place, according to the Gospels.

Jesus stood in the place of God, on the mount, and assumed a divine prerogative to speak on God's behalf with God's authentic voice. This is why the crowds were so astonished: "When Jesus had finished saying these things, the crowds were amazed at his teaching, because he taught as one who had authority, and not as their teachers of the law" (Matt. 7:28). Matthew knew full well that the Torah teachers did teach with authority.[8] What the crowd is saying is that Jesus is one who taught on *His own authority*, one who teaches without citing legal precedent and in His own name interprets the Torah of Moses given by God on Mount Horeb. This is perhaps one of the strongest implicit claims of Jesus's divinity. At Jesus's baptism the Spirit of God descended and anointed Him to do and say the kinds of things that only God would do if He were among us.

Later Jesus will set Himself up as the decisive arbiter of truth, saying, "But you are not to be called 'Rabbi,' for you have only one Master and you are all brothers. And do not call anyone on earth 'father,' for you have one Father, and he is in heaven. Nor are you to be called 'teacher,' for you have one Teacher, the Christ" (Matt. 23:8–10). We have to appreciate this bold claim from the perspective of the Jews, who just had never heard this kind of stuff. Matthew's portrayal of Jesus as the Supreme Teacher of God's people comports well with John's claims that Jesus was the incarnate Word of God who was God and was with God in the beginning (John 1:1).

God's Word, Captured in a Sacred Text

Jesus's authoritative sayings and teachings were captured in a sacred text. Second Timothy 3:16–17 states, "All Scripture is God-breathed and is useful for teaching, rebuking, correcting and training in righteousness, so that the man of God may be thoroughly equipped for every good work." We evangelicals love this passage because it affirms what we believe *about* the Bible. For one thing, it is a sacred Word, unlike anything else that mankind possesses. When Paul told Timothy that he had known the "sacred text from childhood," he meant the Hebrew Scriptures.[9] That collection of writings is special, and by extension this would apply to the New Testament also. The reason we consider the New Testament writings to be Scripture is because they have captured Jesus's teachings for the church and Jesus is the incarnate Word of God. The Holy Spirit was instrumental in inspiring the apostles and their associates.

Furthermore, this passage in Timothy affirms the material sufficiency of Scripture. We evangelicals get a tingle up our fundamentalist spines when we hear that. We like being told that the Bible is the sufficient source for our being equipped for life. "So that the man of God may be thoroughly equipped" means that God's Word is materially sufficient to prepare us for life in God's kingdom. That's the mark of the Spirit on the text. Somehow God's very thoughts and words are captured in it, and they equip us for Christ-likeness.

God's Word, Contextualized in Life

The Spirit wants to teach us Christ's Word in the context of life. What is often missed in the above analysis of God's Word, however, is the reason for the Spirit's presence moving, shaping, and breathing into the minds of the men who first received it. He did this so it would have a practical use. Paul says to Timothy that a direct result of the Scripture's inspiration is its usefulness. This means it actually works in the lives of the people who believe it and live it. The Word teaches them in the context of real life.

God has always been about the business of contextualizing His Word and truth in the lives of people. By contextualization we do not mean compromising. We also do not mean capitulating to false ideas or false teaching. By contextualization we mean to *speak the language of God in the language and the context of the receiving culture.* This is the heart of our missional imperative in Scripture.

This is precisely why, for example, God used the symbol of a tabernacle and temple in the Old Testament. Archaeologists have discovered temples that predate Solomon's by hundreds of years.[10] Yet those temples are largely similar in composition and architecture to the Jewish temple.[11]

Why would that be so?

It's because the ancients spoke the language of the temple, and God speaks the language of the receiving culture. When God wants to say something to the teeming masses of humanity, He doesn't make the crowds learn some special religious language. Languages like Hebrew, Aramaic, and Greek were common in the ancient world when God first spoke through them. Our nature is to codify the past and make a monument of it, forgetting that this orthodox Word was once a living, breathing message to the multitudes in the language of the masses.

God always wants to translate His message into the languages and speech forms of the indigenous population. He goes where they are. He embeds His Spirit-inspired truth in the heart of a believer and stamps that believer's life with the power of eternity. Then He sends that Christian into his culture as a messenger—a prophetic voice announcing that the kingdom is at hand. As soon as God speaks, His goal is always to find a translator—a person who can communicate that message in the common vernacular.

GOD'S WORD FOR THE COMMON MAN

This is precisely why God had the New Testament written in the language of *Koine* Greek. *Koine* is the Greek word for "common." Koine Greek was the *lingua franca,* or the universal language, of the Greco-Roman world in the first century. This is also why the letters of the apostles were immediately copied into every language under the sun and why we have thousands of ancient copies of the New Testament available.[12] This is why the most prominent version of the Bible for a thousand years was called the "Latin Vulgate," the word *vulgate* meaning "vulgar," or "common." It's because God wasn't particularly interested in forcing people to learn some "holy" language, thereby limiting our access to Him. Instead, God sought to disperse the message and proliferate it in as many tongues, customs, and traditions as possible.

The Spirit wants to take God's authentic voice and embed it firmly in your context so that you can live this stuff out. And don't be too quick to judge the various forms that the gospel took when it went out into the Greco-Roman world in the early centuries.

The living and eternal Word of God was incarnated in human form and authorized His followers to capture His teachings in a sacred book, and that same God wanted to contextualize Himself in ancient liturgies, mosaic floor tiles, catacomb paintings, hymns and Gregorian chants, and ancient monasteries. He wanted to invade Roman ingenuity, their tight judicial system, and Greek philosophy.

This same Spirit of life wants to inhabit your modern world too. He wants to be in your smartphone and on your e-reader. He wants to be on your radio and your satellite TV and in your blog. He wants to be in your church and at your neighborhood barbeque and in your cubicle or office. He can't wait to inhabit your conversations, your language, your literature, and your culture. He desires to occupy every niche of your existence until the whole earth, starting with your patch of it, is full of the knowledge of God. N. T. Wright has so aptly stated, "Jesus' resurrection is the beginning of God's new project not to snatch people away from earth to heaven but to colonize earth with the life of heaven."[13] Jesus wants to colonize your life—your world—with His life-giving presence through His living and active Word.

Life happens between your first heartbeat and your last. Between those two events exists all the matted undergrowth—the cogs and thickets and minutia of your life. God wants to inhabit every bit of it, to redeem and reclaim it for His kingdom. And so the only direction to travel is through it, and the only true companion is the mysterious Spirit who presided over that first beat of your heart and who will supervise the last one. He wants to bring Jesus's truth to your situation and breathe on the embers of your knowledge, speaking to you and transforming you through His Word.

Yes, we must be careful not to compromise revealed truth. Yes, we must be careful to follow biblical patterns where biblical patterns emerge. But we must not fail to see this God of contextualization in the Bible, this God who desires to confront culture by inhabiting it, not by creating sectarian structures that retreat from it. He speaks to us out of His eternal Word and into our temporal lives. He arrests us, stops us cold, and then transforms us by the Word and the Spirit. The goal of all good Bible study is communion with the living Spirit that we may thoroughly embed His Word in our lives, that our culture may hear God's voice in us—His living letters.

Don't be so quick to limit God's frequency. Learn His Word and fill your mind and heart with His truth. Do your homework. Then let His Spirit surface the Scriptures' principles in the alcoves and inlets and nooks of your daily existence.

9
THE EXTRA-NATURAL POWER OF GOD
The Spirit works through the ordinary.

> Before our spiritual eyes are opened, the world is
> only thirteen inches in diameter. It's like we live
> in a low-definition, two-dimensional world. Then
> the Holy Spirit gives us depth perception. He
> opens our eyes to see the ordinary miracles that
> surround us, the ordinary miracles that are us.[1]
> —MARK BATTERSON—
> *Primal*

ORDINARY.

Kind of a depressing word, isn't it? Not because the word conjures images of searing defeat or epic failure. "Ordinary" is such an uninspired term. I mean, no one ever celebrated the game-winning buzzer-beater by jumping up and shouting, "Yay! We won! We are *so ordinary!* We are the *most adequate* team in history!"

And certain words just sound like their dictionary definitions, don't they? Like the word *mediocre*. Whenever I hear the word *mediocre*, I can't help but picture a lukewarm bowl of tasteless mush. You get the picture. Now close your eyes and slowly say it with me: "me-di-o-cre." Did you feel the unexceptional quality of that word just wash over you?

Or how about the term *pizazz!* Now *that's* a word with some texture. This word has some snap to it. It pops. The word even looks like it's in motion zipping across the page. Yeah, some words just capture the imagination better than others.

But back to the word *ordinary*. Though it is a word intended to describe the status quo, it is truly one of the most important concepts in Christianity. Because, as it turns out, God's Spirit specializes in using normal things, the everyday stuff, to do His sovereign bidding. It turns out that ordinary is just the sort of neutral canvas that God uses when He wants to wow us with His awesomeness.

FEARFULLY AND WONDERFULLY ORDINARY

It just so happens that there are some really great reasons to believe in the existence of the supernatural, not the least of which is the natural world itself. This universe appears to operate with clockwork precision. What we think of as ordinary creation turns out to be some of the most miraculous, extraordinary stuff imaginable.

Just take, for example, the laws of physics. Did you know that the universe is governed by a delicately synchronized set of physical constants? In their book entitled *The Privileged Planet*, authors Guillermo Gonzalez and Jay Richards show that laws like gravity, the electromagnetic force, the speed of light, the mass density of the universe, the strong and weak nuclear forces—all operate on the edge of a razor.[2] Dial the force of gravity a click to the right, or change the cosmological constants to any degree—and the universe would not be life permitting. It's staggering to think just how fearfully and wonderfully our universe is made.

Or take, for example, the issue of our planet's habitability.[3] Even though the physical constants are like perfectly synchronized cogs in a clock, the universe is still hostile to life unless some very specific conditions are met. Gonzalez and Richards point out that in order to have a life-permitting planet in the universe, it would need to be a planet with just the right location in the solar system. We are in what is known as the Goldilocks zone—not too hot, not too cold; we are just the right distance from the sun.

A life-permitting planet would also have to be in a just the right "circumstellar sweet spot," or a habitable zone of the solar system.[4] It would need to be in a system with giant planetary bodies to shield it from the harmful space debris in the universe. This planet would need to orbit just the right kind of star that gives off just the right kind of radiation. It would need to be a planet with a moon to stabilize the tilt of its axis. It would have to be a terrestrial (land-dwelling) world that is just the right size. If the earth were smaller, the magnetic field would be too weak, which would result in the sun's solar wind stripping away our atmosphere. It would have to have just the right amount of internal spin and heat so that it could generate just the right magnetic field.[5] There would have to be a perfect mixture of nitrogen, oxygen, and carbon dioxide, with just the right water-to-land ratio, allowing for the complex overlap between so many ecosystems. A life-permitting planet would have to be nestled in a solar system that is in a particularly uncrowded spot in our galaxy where habitability is optimized but the threats to us are minimized.[6]

This is just a sampling of the many specific conditions that would need to be met in order to make a planet habitable—and the earth just happens to meet them perfectly. Life on earth is balanced on a razor's edge. Our universe, our world, is a first-rate miracle of God. There is no reason why we should exist, and there is every reason why we shouldn't. Yet God has etched the message of His existence from the largest galaxies right down to the smallest particles of matter. And the fact that I can ponder its meaning is itself evidence for this supernatural Creator. C. S. Lewis put it this way:

> My argument against God was that the universe seemed
> so cruel and unjust. But how had I got this idea of *just*
> and *unjust*?…If the whole universe has no meaning, we
> should never have found out that it has no meaning: just

as, if there were no light in the universe and therefore no creatures with eyes, we would never know that it was dark. *Dark* would be a word without meaning.[7]

If the universe were not designed, then it wouldn't be orderly. If it were not orderly, it would not be intelligible, and if it were not intelligible, it would not be discoverable. The assumption that the universe is orderly and discoverable is what makes science possible. It's also what makes worship possible.

It turns out that the ordinary isn't so ordinary after all. Every natural miracle in our world points us to a supernatural God.

Baked-In Potential

If I asked you what was the first miracle in the Bible, what would be your answer? Hang on, I'm going to ask my kids. I'll be right back…

OK, I asked them. The answers ranged from Noah's flood to the crossing of the Red Sea. What would your answer be? I imagine that most of us will gravitate toward the first few chapters of Genesis. Noah's flood is definitely a good candidate. But the answer is actually Genesis 1:1—"In the beginning God created the heavens and the earth." That's the first supernatural thing God ever did.

God's first miracle was to create the natural world. This Creation account is what we refer to as an ancient "cosmology," or a story of origins.[8] Genesis is one of many Creation accounts in the ancient world, including Babylonian, Sumerian, and Egyptian stories that sought to explain the origin of our world. But there are three radical ideas that distinguish the Hebrew account from all these others.

First, God has no origin.

Unlike the deities of the pagan world, God is transcendent, meaning His existence is not tied to creation—He isn't a contingent being. God's existence is categorically different from anything else in all creation. He isn't the sun god because He was begat from the sun. And He's not the fertility god because He was born out of the river and the marsh. This God stands apart from the natural world and is not tied to its existence in any way. The unmistakable inference of Genesis 1:1 is that before beginning began, God *was*. And Jesus told us that "God is spirit" (John 4:24). He isn't material. He's something entirely "other." The ancient Hebrews had a way of saying that God was "other." They used the word *holy*.

Second, the Spirit was instrumental in creation.

This Genesis cosmology shows us that the Spirit of God was instrumental in bringing all natural phenomena—everything in the spectrum of creation—into being. The Spirit was there "hovering over the waters" (Gen. 1:2). The Spirit of God was an active agent in the formation of the basic elements of the world.[9] God supervised it and sustains it by His powerful Word (Heb. 1:3). I sometimes hear people talk of the Holy Spirit as if His first appearance (and His last appearance, for that matter) was on the Day of Pentecost. Not true. The Spirit of God was present as the primal elements of nature began to take shape and come into existence.

Third, mankind's role in the world is ordinary.

God breathed the Spirit's life into the man's nostrils. Man was made to commune with God in nature. In fact, he was made to commune with God *au naturel*. He was made for the earth. He is the likeness of God—which means he is God's representative in the biosphere where he's been placed. God's responsibilities for him are primarily *ordinary*. He's supposed to cultivate his farm. He's supposed to responsibly develop natural resources and multiply his progeny across the face of the earth.[10]

He has some parameters too. He can make use of all the livestock; he can eat of every tree except one. He can till the soil, farm the land, build a house, raise a town, and expand into a city.

None of this is off-limits to him. In fact, all of it is part of his job description. He is supposed to commune with the God who is Spirit in the midst of a world that is supernaturally natural.

Let me ask you a pointed question: Do you view your life, your job, and your work as stuff that God isn't all that interested in? Do you tend to view church matters like prophecy, visions, dreams, and speaking in tongues as the really important stuff, while all that punching a clock, taking care of kids, and being a responsible neighbor—well, that's just the "worldly" stuff. I've got news for you: God made you for that worldly stuff. Not worldly in the sense of the world's value system though. I mean earthly. God made you for earth life. The Spirit wants to inhabit your life. He wants to redeem and consecrate the mundane stuff of tending gardens, naming animals, building communities, and having kids.

So it should come as no surprise that God wants to interact with the natural world that He has supernaturally created. He hasn't spun it up and left the scene. God still does amazing things—and often He accomplishes His work by partnering with the wonderfully ordinary laws He's already put in place. The potential for wonderful exploits is already baked into the creation.

The same Spirit that brooded over the face of the elements in Genesis wants to continue hovering over every detail of your otherwise mundane and ordinary existence. To be sure, God wants to give you some dreams and visions and do powerful miracles for you and through you on occasion. But for the most part, He wants to walk with you through the endless ordinary.

SUPERNATURAL AND EXTRA-NATURAL

Every time the deity from the Hebrew Scriptures interacts with the natural world, He employs laws He's already put into place. I refer to this as the extra-natural power of God. It is God working within this ecosystem, within its laws and limitations, that is so fascinating to me. And this pattern occurs from cover to cover of your Bible. In fact, the Spirit interacting with the natural stuff is the normative pattern in Scripture.

We've already mentioned the Flood, so let's start there. This is probably the biggest miracle story post-garden in Genesis. When we look closely at the story, we see that God wants a giant boat built, so He has Noah and his sons slog away and build it. He doesn't make it magically appear out of thin air. When He wants to actually flood the earth, He doesn't lean over the sky and weep giant God-tears, filling up the oceans. Instead He pops open the springs, shifts around some tectonic plates, and sends the rain. The point is that this miracle was a partnership between the world that God had already supernaturally created and His presence. This is what distinguishes the biblical accounts from ancient mythologies such as the *Epic of Gilgamesh*.

God speaks to the inner ear of a human being made in His image—to Noah. God gives him specific directions. God triggers the rain and the upsurge of water and safeguards the ark until it reaches its destination. God's fingerprints are all over the scene. But He doesn't sidestep His miraculous world—He uses it. Our problem is that we have become so accustomed to the extraordinary world that surrounds us.

So the sun rises and sets like clockwork every day, and we assume that it *should* do that. But the only reason why it *should* do that is because God wills it so. Every time it appears, it is an absolute miracle. Each night when that dazzling glowing orb disappears into the horizon, it does so because God has decreed it. It operates naturally within the framework set for it by a supernatural Creator.

Here's Mud in Your Eye

Let's fast-forward to one of my favorite miracles of Jesus. It is the miracle of healing the blind man with spit and dirt.

Now surely Jesus did things that are truly supernatural in the sense that He sidestepped natural laws. People don't frequently walk on water, change the molecular composition of H_2O to grape juice, and vanish like a vapor through walls the way Jesus did. Getting up and walking out of a tomb after a hellish beating and crucifixion as if awakening from a nap is the sort of thing that only God could do. So for sure, there are extraordinary miracles in Jesus's life that can't and shouldn't be ignored.

But some of my favorite scenes are those moments when Jesus, as a Spirit-filled man, interacts with the limitations of human medicinal aids and resources. I'm thinking specifically of when Jesus healed the blind man on the Sabbath. In the story Jesus is treating the ailment like a Jewish charismatic sage. He is using a medicinal aid that was expressly forbidden to be used on the Sabbath according to the oral Torah—the ancestral traditions of the Pharisees.[11] Yet Jesus is complying with the written Scriptures and heals the man using dirt, salve, and water. Jesus forms a muddy sealant—rubbing the grimy concoction on the blind man's swarthy and dry skin. Sometimes God wants to use the natural elements to assist His supernatural work.

"Go wash it off."

The blind man is led to the pool. With a few splashes of water, the muddy grout dissolves and retinal tissue is reborn. Optic nerves spontaneously regenerate. The visual center of his brain floods with light, color, movement—and *Jesus*.

Whether it was infusing medicinal remedies with the Spirit's power or exponentially multiplying pickled fish and flat bread for a hillside of growling stomachs, Jesus's miracles strike me as a beautiful partnership between the Spirit's power and the natural world that He supernaturally created. Jesus can suspend natural laws, or He can employ and enhance them.

ONE OF THESE MIRACLES IS NOT LIKE THE OTHER

Not too long ago I discovered that I have stenosis in my neck. I had been praying for over two years about this issue and had asked God repeatedly to take the pain away. It was getting to the point of being unbearable. I had gone to several doctors and chiropractors who all misdiagnosed my condition. I finally went to a physiatrist and a neurologist who correctly diagnosed my problem and prescribed a plan of care that included a certain kind of medication that brought the swelling down and a regular physical health routine of stretching, exercise, and weight loss to take the pressure off of my upper body. It worked. In fact, it has worked so well that I am putting off a neck fusion that the neurologist suggested I undergo. The doctor was an answer to my prayer. Thank God for that brilliant physician. Thank God for a world well stocked with natural cures and treatments to common ailments.

Now, I've had other circumstances where the Spirit of the Lord healed me instantly as a result of someone else's prayer. One particular situation required me to have surgery, and so I was scheduled to go in. My family laid hands on me and prayed that God would take away the pain, and the problem went away instantly. It has never recurred.

Which of these circumstances would you call a miracle? I hope by now your answer would be "both," because God supernaturally made the laws of physics, gave men intellect and wisdom, and gave us the raw materials to develop medicinal aids and cures for life's illnesses. God is no less the author of that than He is the author of my instantaneous healing. God is a fan of healing *and health.*

If Jesus could use salve and mud and water and infuse those natural elements with His miracle-working power, if God could use the tectonic plates cracking open to send a miraculous flood, then surely He can use your doctor to heal your body or to prescribe medicine that will take the edge off. Every last bit of it brings Him glory, because absolutely none of it should exist in the first place. God is the author of both the supernatural and the extra-natural, and He will use whatever means at your disposal to help you and to test and refine your faith.

A REALLY LATE PAYCHECK

Years ago, before I went off to college, I had landed a job working construction for a summer. I had worked the entire season and was due to collect my paycheck as a poor, struggling college student. However, the gentleman wouldn't pay up. So not only did I lose out on the money, but also I lost the opportunity to work somewhere else for the entire summer. I went off to school and quickly found another job and eventually forgot about the matter.

Years later, after graduating from college, my wife and I spent a few years in youth ministry at a church in the Tri-Cities, Washington. But then we felt God calling us to help my friend Steve plant a church in Minnesota. So we sent out a letter to everyone we knew, asking for help with travel costs. Our letter spelled out our vision, and many people gave and supported us in this amazing adventure.

However, one of the individuals to whom I had sent the letter wasn't so thrilled about this cold call for support. His return letter ripped into me. Not only did he critique every detail of my "crummy" letter, but he also questioned my audacity to ask him for help. The letter cut me deep because it was the same individual who had stiffed me years earlier.

"This guy really just doesn't like me," I thought.

Then, out of the envelope fell a $600 check. Despite his ire and pensive attitude, he felt moved to give anyway. Turns out it was exactly the amount we needed to put the deposit down on our rental van and cover the last of our travel costs. In fact, his gift was the largest single check that we received from anyone. It also happened to be the *exact* amount he owed me for the summer I worked for him years earlier.

That was a miracle, because it was exactly what we needed, when we needed it. It didn't look like the Mount of Transfiguration in Matthew 17, and it didn't look like a vision of a sheet letting down from heaven and hearing an audible voice from the sky. But it was a miracle nonetheless. It looked more like fish and loaves and mud getting rubbed into the eyes of the blind. And God used someone who didn't even like me to accomplish His will.

I could tell you many stories like that. But I'll leave it there. My question to you is this: Do you believe that God can use your neighbor, your doctor, your world, and even your enemy to help you? If you believe that God is the Creator of all things, you should be open to the possibility that He wants to bless you supernaturally and extra-naturally.

Open your eyes to the marvelous stage set and props that God has built for your story. Open your imagination to how He might bless you and help you in your journey through the very world He spoke into existence and mashed and shaped together by His Spirit. The same Holy Spirit that created every subatomic particle of the universe is available to inhabit your situation—to multiply your mere provisions or to rub healing on your dark and weary eyes.

The Drabber the Canvas, the Greater the Glory

What we've seen in this chapter is that God performs the supernatural. He can do anything He wants. But He often works through the natural order that He's already created. In the next chapter we'll get more specific about what this looks like in the local church. It turns out that God's Spirit has equipped the church with spiritual gifts—some of these gifts are enhanced natural abilities, and others are supernatural and somewhat spectacular. But don't be too quick to disparage the ordinary—your ordinary job, your ordinary house, or your ordinary kids. God specializes in using ordinary stuff to do amazing things.

After all, the apostles were unschooled, ordinary men who turned the world upside down in the power of the Spirit. Stephen in the Book of Acts was just an ordinary deacon who didn't even have a preaching job. But he was filled with the Holy Spirit and power and died a glorious death for the Savior. Our ordinary lives are just the sort of drab canvasses that God uses to bring Himself great glory as He accomplishes amazing things in you by His Spirit.

10

RED-SHIRT CHRISTIANS

The Spirit gives us significance.

> For one receives the spirit of understanding,
> another the spirit of counsel, another the spirit of
> might, another the spirit of healing, another the
> spirit of prophecy, another the spirit of doctrine,
> and another the spirit of the fear of God.[1]
> —JUSTIN MARTYR—
> (AD 150)

BACK BEFORE THE days when television sets came with remote controls, my dad devised an ingenious system to change the channels remotely. He called this system "children." While he lay on the couch with a cigarette in his mouth and a beer on the coffee table, he'd tell me to get up and stand by the TV.

"Adjust the antenna to the left, Jeffrey." I'd move the rabbit ear antennas, trying to find that sweet spot, and then, "Got it. Stop right there. Now turn the station until I say stop."

I didn't much like being a human remote control. But fortunately there were only three channels to choose from back in the 1970s. Those old TV sets had thick plastic dials called "channel selectors." Finding a new program required a solid twist of the wrist in order to ratchet the channel selector left or right. *Clunk-clunk! Clunk-clunk!* I'd cycle through the three channels until Daddy found a show he wanted to watch. To his credit, he would often land on a program that he knew we'd all stay in the room to watch together.

Our all-time favorite show was the cult classic *Star Trek*. The series didn't last long in the 1960s when it first appeared. But by the 1970s *Star Trek* was in syndication and the reruns were playing constantly. So each night I'd get up and... *Clunk-clunk! Clunk-clunk!* Surf the three channels until I landed on *Star Trek*.

I was instantly mesmerized by this classic show. I wanted to be Captain Kirk and command the starship *Enterprise*. I wanted to spend my life as an intrepid explorer, voyaging through space, going on away missions, meeting new aliens, killing Klingons— all with inspiring theme music playing in the background. I once even prayed when I was a kid, "God, I hope when I die that my eternal heavenly reward involves getting my own starship so I can fly at warp speed around the new heavens and the new earth. In Jesus's name, amen." My goal in life was to become Captain Awesome.

THE EXPENDABLES

After watching the first twenty episodes of Star *Trek*, I began to notice certain patterns in the show. Almost every episode had a crisis of cosmic scope where the spaceship *Enterprise* was threatened with destruction and Kirk and Spock had to figure out an ingenious solution.

At just the right moment in the show when the captain's unlikely plan was facing failure due to impossible odds, engineer Scotty would somehow deliver "more power" from those already taxed warp engines, even though he swore that he had already given the captain "all she's got." Spock would remark how all this was fascinating, McCoy would declare that he was a doctor and not a brick layer, and Kirk would always get the girl.

And no episode would be complete without an away team beaming down to the planet surface. The away teams usually consisted of Kirk in a khaki shirt, Spock and McCoy in blue shirts, and a couple of security guards in red shirts. I noticed that the red-shirt security officers almost never came back from away missions. Their obvious purpose on the show was to heighten the threat level. The bad guys would kill off the red-shirts, which established that the threat to the main characters was real. The main characters always seemed to be smart enough or fortunate enough to cheat death. But those poor red-shirt guys just couldn't keep up. At some point the show's creators decided that the red-shirts were expendable. These disposable extras existed to prop up the stars. In fact, the red-shirt guys usually didn't even have names.

In the same way the Christian church is rife with this kind of red-shirt mentality. Somehow we've gotten in our minds that the masses exist to prop up a few, fortunate, and gifted starlets so that they can accomplish the miraculous or so that they can achieve big things for the kingdom. We noted earlier that Paul forbade this undue regard for human leaders in his letter to the Corinthians. Beyond this observation, we must point out that it is OK to give leaders their due honor, and Paul recognizes this elsewhere. Spiritually mature believers have a natural role of leadership in the life of the local church, and it's appropriate to recognize this. That said, when it comes to the issue of giftedness, Paul made it clear that no one is expendable in God's household.

Extra Grace

God has given all believers Spirit manifestations, or gifts, and all believers, both Jews and Gentiles, now participate in the building of the kingdom of God on earth. The word for *gifts* in the New Testament is *charis*, which is the Greek word for "grace." We receive Jesus's grace at salvation, but then the Spirit gives us extra grace to empower us for service. This is the kingdom agenda.

This program for humanity is called "ministry." Contrary to the popular use of the term, "ministry" is not for a select group of people. Ministry is for all believers. Paul told the Ephesians that the preacher's job is to outfit all believers for ministry in God's kingdom (Eph. 4:11–12). But before Paul encouraged the Jewish and Gentile Christians in Rome to discover and deploy their spiritual gifts, he spelled out the qualifications for every believer. Though there are some specialized requirements for certain ministries, the following are Paul's qualifications for all believers in discovering their spiritual ministry in the body of Christ.

Ministry starts with right living. Paul asserted that the Roman Christians' first task was to align their priorities and their lifestyle with kingdom values as they surrender to God in well-reasoned worship. He stated, "I appeal to you therefore, brothers, by the mercies of God, to present your bodies as a living sacrifice, holy and acceptable to God, which is your spiritual worship" (Rom. 12:1, ESV). After establishing that mankind is altogether lost (Rom. 1–3), he makes his case for justification by grace through faith alone (Rom. 3–5). This salvation experience is an empowering grace, which has severed our ties to sin, broken sin's power over us (Rom. 6–7), and has now enabled us to walk in the newness of life by the Spirit (Rom. 8). This salvation is the gospel to both the Jews and Gentiles (Rom. 9–11). And now both people groups (Jew and Gentile) must continually walk in the newness of Spirit life, empowered to serve the body of Christ through Spirit graces, or what we call "spiritual gifts" (Rom. 12).

BARGAIN SACRIFICES

Ministry involves costly obedience. Contemporary believers just have no grid through which to understand the importance of sacrifice in the ancient world. Paul calling our lives a "living sacrifice" was truly a novel idea. Ancient sacrifice was a messy enterprise, and worshippers were required to bring their best offering. Moses commanded the Jews, "You will be accepted only if your offering is a male animal with no defects. It may be a bull, a ram, or a male goat." (See Leviticus 1:1–3, NLT.) This commitment to pure sacrifices was engrained in their Jewish culture. Bringing blemished or diseased lambs or weak and scrawny cattle to be slaughtered at the temple was unthinkable in the first century. Whether you brought the offering or bought the offering, either way, sacrificing the "best" would cost you something. It wasn't cheap.

But "cheap" is a deeply rooted American value. Even the word *value* has been hijacked and has become a synonym for "cheap." I love to take my wife out for the occasional splurge on an expensive meal. But most of the time I'm content with a dollar hot dog at Costco. I also occasionally break the budget for a nice article of clothing, but I usually shop at discount stores. And I confess that even in discount stores I'm looking at the clearance rack or the scratch-and-dent shelf. (I told you I was cheap.) I live for a good value. I believe frugality is a virtue, not a vice. But my obsession with value at a low cost to me, the consumer, is inherently at war with my life of spiritual sacrifice. Paul expected us to view our very bodies, and our very selves, as the living, realized temple of God (1 Cor. 3:10; 1 Cor. 6; 2 Cor. 5). This involves extravagant worship as we give ourselves completely to Him. *God is not the least bit interested in the chump change of bargain-basement offerings.*

Before Paul jumped into the issue of Spirit gifts, he wanted to make sure the Romans knew that they all, Jew and Gentile alike, had received the Spirit, and this means they were to be walking, talking, living sacrifices.

BE TRANSFORMED

Ministry flows from a transformed heart. Paul continued, "Do not be conformed to this world, but be transformed by the renewal of your mind, that by testing you may discern what is the will of God, what is good and acceptable and perfect" (Rom. 12:2, ESV). Perhaps the single most frequent question a pastor will get is how to discover God's "will for my life." Often people ask me this, hoping that I will have some kind of deep prophetic insight or perhaps a word of knowledge about their future. Without failure I will lead them to this passage.

And almost no one wants to hear it because it isn't particularly impressive. No apocalyptic dreams are needed for discovering God's will—just the homespun advice of trial and error—you test and approve God's revealed will in your particular circumstance. Paul did not tell the Romans to "discover" the will of God for their lives. Instead he told them to "test and approve" the already revealed will of God. Though we'll have more to say about this in a later chapter on purity, we want to establish now that it is God's will for you to be holy. And it is God's will for you to engage with your spiritual gifts in ministry. Until you are doing that—don't bother asking God for your dream spouse or your dream job. Live holy and plug in to your local church—then seek Him for the specifics.

God is omnipresent, meaning His presence is everywhere all the time. There is nowhere where He isn't. But a temple is a place where God's *manifest* presence rests. The Hebrew word for this idea of a deity resting in a temple was *shevat*, where we get the word *Sabbath*. That's what deities did in the ancient world—they rested in their temples.[2]

The temple is also where that deity displays his power through his priesthood. But Paul taught that every believer and the church corporately are the living temple of God. That temple is the place where God's Spirit dwells among men. That's where God displays His power. That's where God shows His stuff and reveals what He can do in an ordinary human life.

We are the place where heaven and earth overlap. We are the nexus between two worlds. Wright puts it this way, "Those in whom the Spirit comes to live are God's new temple. They are, individually and corporately, places where heaven and earth meet."[3] So what kind of behavior ought to accompany a person who is a living holy place indwelt by the Holy Spirit? Naturally, it is holy living as the Spirit transforms you into the image of Jesus.

A Wondrous Dread

We discover our ministry through accurate self-assessment. Paul goes on to say to the Romans, "Do not think of yourself more highly than you ought, but rather think of yourself with sober judgment, in accordance with the measure of faith God has given you" (Rom. 12:3). No one is more self-unaware than a drunken fool. There's a reason why they call it "liquid courage." Because when you're half-lit—you are way out of touch with your limits. You think you can drive and you can't even find your keys. You flail away in a barroom fight and you can barely stand up. You imagine yourself to be hot stuff, when in reality you are a drunken, stinking mess who needs to go sleep it off and get a shower.

Paul told the Romans that they needed "sober judgment," or accurate self-assessment. This means we need to be in touch with our levels, with our limits, and with our passions. Know thyself.

When I first recommitted my life to Jesus as a teenager, I thought for sure God wanted me to be a healing evangelist like Reinhard Bonnke. Bonnke's fiery preaching seemed to be touched by heaven itself. I thought for sure that was God's will for me. However, the Spirit had other plans. As I prayed and sought the Lord, the Holy Spirit revealed Himself in an unusual way.

That's putting it mildly.

As a teenager, one Friday evening I knelt on the floor of my room and opened my NIV Study Bible on the bed. I began singing and worshipping God, and that's when it happened. God's presence invaded my space. I fell on the floor unable to move. The presence of the Spirit was so powerful in those moments that it felt like the spatiotemporal world had zipped open, allowing the glory of God to flood the room where I was kneeling. It was a feeling of awe, wonder, bliss, and terror all rolled into one experience. I sensed that I was in the presence of a Being who could command the very elements of nature—a Being who could speak and the very cloth of the natural world would respond instantly to His sovereign will. This experience inspired a wondrous dread in me.

In that moment as I lay stunned under the power of the Spirit, suddenly God poured into my soul a rapacious hunger for His living Word. The more I worshipped, the more this hunger filled me. I wanted to know His truth so badly that I thought I would burst. Try as I might, the experience is just indescribable. But it was in that moment that God birthed in me a desire for what I believe is a scholarly knowledge of His Word. Now, God isn't too impressed with scholarly knowledge. For that matter, God isn't too impressed with rocket science or Einstein's theory of general relativity, either. I'm sure God is pleasantly amused at all of our "advanced" sciences and disciplines.

But that is the moment when a gift and hunger for wisdom and godly knowledge entered me. And I have never been the same. It is an unquenchable fire in my very self. I want to help believers experience a love that overflows as they grow in knowledge and depth of insight into God's truth (Phil. 1:9). Before that moment I was a high-school dropout. I entered college on academic probation. But I went on to get four post-secondary degrees, graduating magna cum laude with the last four of them. Before I received the gift, I had no desire for it, no hunger for knowledge growth. After I received the gift, I couldn't turn it off. I still can't.

As it turns out, I haven't preached in foreign lands that much. And I haven't performed very many physical healings at the direction of the Lord, either. Not that I didn't try. In my earlier days I had to help a lot of crippled people back into their wheelchairs after praying for them.

My desire to be a healing evangelist was not answered. God had another path for me. And I am serving Him with those gifts. Now, my gifts and calling aren't any less important than those of Billy Graham or Reinhard Bonnke, which leads us to our final observation about Spirit graces from the Romans passage. After Paul told the Romans they needed to view themselves with sober judgment, he wanted every believer to discover their unique spiritual contribution to the body of Christ.

What's Your Function?

Every believer is gifted for Spirit ministry. Paul continues his argument, "For as in one body we have many members, and the members do not all have the same function, so we, though many, are one body in Christ, and individually members one of another. Having gifts that differ according to the grace given to us, let us use them" (Rom. 12:4–6, esv). Notice that last phrase, "Let us use them." We see in this passage that the Spirit graces have a functional purpose (v. 4), are of varying types, like different body parts (v. 5), and they should be employed not forbidden. My favorite word in those three verses is the word *function.* This is because I have seen a lot of dysfunctional Christianity in my day. Paul used this term together with the analogy of a body with many functioning parts.

This is exactly why marriages and families implode and relationships self-destruct. It's because the members of that family are not performing their function. Paul taught that husbands and wives are to submit to one another out of reverence for Jesus (Eph. 5:21). Men are supposed to submit to their wives by sacrificing themselves the way Jesus did for the church (v. 25). Women are supposed to submit to their husbands by voluntarily serving the way the church gives itself for Jesus (v. 24). But when men don't perform their function, they ruin their marriages. When they're selfish, lazy, lustful, and refuse to submit through sacrifice, then they blow up their relationships. And when women don't submit through service and mutual respect, then they fail to fulfill their function. The result is malfunction.

The same is true for children. When kids are allowed to run roughshod over their parents in disrespect, when children become indulged little terrors—families suffer for it. It's because parts of the family aren't functioning—they're not performing

their intended role. Again, this always leads to dysfunction. This
is why Paul tells the Romans that every person needs to operate
according to their gifts. Because this is the only way the body, the
family of Christ, can operate as it was intended.

YOU'RE NOT AN EXTRA

So when, for example, you see a church that is dominated by
one charismatic superstar who treats everyone else like expendable "red-shirts," then you are witnessing a fatally flawed, glitchy
church paradigm. Conversely, whenever you see a congregation
without godly leaders who prophetically speak into the lives of
the church, then again you're witnessing a dysfunctional church
family. Though there are varying degrees of gifts in each local
body, and though there are some gifts that are more helpful in
building community than others, *everyone* has something to con-
tribute. *No one* is expendable in Jesus's household. All believers
play a critical role in the expansion of God's kingdom message
into the world.

God doesn't have any red-shirts on His team. You aren't disposable, and you're not an extra in God's kingdom plot. You have
great worth and value to God. But the prerequisite to discovering
and deploying your gifts is a pursuit of holiness resulting in inner
transformation, sober self-assessment, and an open heart.

11

SPIRIT-GIFTED LOVE MACHINES
The Spirit unleashed from a heart of love

Love never fails.[1]
—PAUL—
Every Christian would agree that a man's spiritual
health is exactly proportional to his love for God.[2]
—C. S. LEWIS—

WHEN WE WERE kids, my brother and I went out into the forest and found a bunch of logs that had been cut to make a path for power lines. My brother got the bright idea to take those logs and build a fort. So we got Dad's ax and hatchet and began to cut notches into the ends of the wood, and then we stacked them in log-cabin fashion.

With the logs about four feet high, we stepped back and realized that this fort was looking awesome, so we kept going until we had built the cabin to about seven feet. Finally we cut some old pine branches to make a thatch roof. When it was done, we inspected the cabin fort, congratulating ourselves on this monument to our ingenuity. Then we realized we'd forgotten to build a door into it. There was no way to actually get into the log fort.

So we got out some shovels and dug a wide trench—tunneling our way into the cabin. We spent the whole day in our new fort in disbelief at how cool and awesome it was. The next day we went to get our neighbor friends to show them our log tower. We talked it up the whole way there. But we were alarmed to discover that the cabin had collapsed overnight and was lying in a heap. I estimate about six hundred to eight hundred pounds of fresh cut logs were piled in the spot where we'd played the day before.

So we rebuilt it.

The problem was that we'd built the fort on a faulty foundation. Not only was the ground uneven, but also we dug a "hole door," which undermined the stability of our structure. We told our dad what had happened, and he suggested a more excellent way—build your fort on a level, solid foundation.

In the same way we observed that the Corinthian Christians in the first century had built something too. It was a flashy church with lots of cool things going on. They excelled in many Spirit gifts and didn't lack any Spirit ability. In fact, Paul stated they would have these gifts available until Jesus Himself returned (1 Cor. 1:7, ESV). God had richly supplied them with lots of spontaneous Spirit manifestations, and it had gotten Paul's attention. Unfortunately they hadn't taken the time to construct this flashy church on a solid foundation of mutual concern and care. Paul challenged them to build their lives on the bedrock of Christian love, which was the more excellent way (1 Cor. 12:31).

TOOLS OR ART?

To this day I still have a fascination with building stuff. However, I'm not very good at it. Plus, all my tools are whack anyway. I have the typical garage wall pegboard with some screwdrivers, a few pliers, a wrench or two, a couple of clamps, and a mixed bag of various bolts. So, not surprisingly when I make a trip over to the local hardware "mall," I stand in the aisles and drool. I gawk at the hardware like a sophisticated metrosexual strolling the aisles of a fine New York art gallery. These stores have miles of product and every tool imaginable. And I have a special place for each of them in my man heart.

My favorite section in the hardware store is the power tool department. I salivate over portable power saws, pneumatic nail drivers, and belt sanders. Whenever I am in this section, I can't help but eagerly desire everything on the wall. On my way out I breathe a quick prayer of repentance for the lust in my heart for these beautiful works of tool art.

But that's just it. They're not art pieces, and the hardware store is not a museum. Art is produced purely for aesthetic value. Art was made to be appreciated, not used. But tools are different. Tools are designed with a function. They are made to help you make something. In the same way, spiritual gifts are power tools and not works of art. They weren't meant to be observed or appreciated for their own sake. They were intended to help us construct the kingdom of God on earth with the Spirit's power. Their purpose is to build lives. Their purpose is to reinforce a local kingdom outpost—to build up the people within it so they may fulfill their obligations to love God passionately and to love others selflessly.

And I need these tools because I am a deeply flawed creature who requires God's almightiness. When God equips me, He puts His gifts in the hands of a defective instrument—a man who is in progress and in need of the daily grace and power of the Spirit.

Noisy Moppets

But these spiritual tools are worthless or even reckless in the hands of a loveless churchgoer. Paul wanted us to wield these gifts with a heart of mutual concern and love. Paul sums up his argument concerning Spirit graces, or Spirit gifts, in one simple sentence: "Follow the way of love and eagerly desire spiritual gifts, especially the gift of prophecy" (1 Cor. 14:1). Paul sought to balance their use of Spirit gifts with an emphasis on God's love.

He did not want the Corinthians to be ignorant of Spirit gifts (1 Cor. 12:1). Instead he wanted them to be informed regarding their nature and proper operation. Paul asserted that there were a variety of gifts—like tributaries shooting off of a main riverbed—but the same Spirit was the fountainhead of them all (v. 4). These gifts were manifestations, or exhibitions of the Spirit's power in their midst (v. 6). They were intended for the mutual encouragement and support of Christ's body (v. 7) and ranged from *native abilities* like service, administration, and generosity (v. 5; Rom. 12:7), to *nonnative abilities* such as gifts of healings, miracles, and heavenly speech forms (1 Cor. 12:9–11; 14:9–14; Rom. 12:6). Paul encouraged them to eagerly desire the greater gifts (1 Cor. 14:1), that is, gifts that contributed to the collective good (v. 12). The best gift is the one you need. The best tool is the one that fits your job. If you're in corporate worship— you need prophecy, teaching, and service. When you're alone, you need inspired speech, knowledge, and insight.

The Corinthian believers needed a sure footing on the bedrock of Christian love (1 Cor. 13). Paul argued that no one wins in a super-charged worship service where selfishness abounds. Without love, the most spectacular gifts are nothing more than the racket of a spiritual nursery—immature and undeveloped believers who clang around on their toys like a bunch of babbling, self-centered moppets (vv. 1–3). That is an unstable foundation on which to build the kingdom.

Let's pause to explore the true nature of love.

QUICKSAND MONSTER

When they were really little, I used to love throwing my kids around on the bed or the couch. Listening to them belly-laugh as they hurled through the air and landed safely on a soft mattress or a cushy couch was one of my favorite things to do.

My kids' favorite game is called "Quicksand Monster." The game is very simple, and it is an automatic scream and giggle fest in my house. I lie on the floor as the quicksand monster. The kids try to run across the living room without getting caught in the "quicksand." I catch one of them and pull him or her closer to me while squeezing tight. Then the other three jump in to save the poor wretch who has fallen into the clutches of old quicksand monster. The kids struggle and work to free their sister or brother, but the one who saves is the one who gets caught and pulled into the bog. My kids could literally play this game all day long. They never get tired of it.

You see, my kids don't love me because I walk in the door at night and put my bag down and decree throughout the home, "Children! Thy father is home. Thou shalt commence loving me." No such decrees are necessary. My kids love me because I wrestle on the floor and throw them end over end across the couch. Loving a father is natural. And loving our heavenly Father is also natural.

The way of love begins with what C. S. Lewis called an "appetite for God." We develop a passionate appetite for God as we loiter in His presence. God is not looking for thrifty worshippers—churchgoers who are on a tight schedule. They need to get straight to the lecture with no foreplay of heart. They need the drive-by version because they have other things to do and other places to be. He doesn't want to be an entry on our schedule. The Spirit is looking for people who take pleasure in lingering in His presence. Mike Bickle writes:

> In our day, the Holy Spirit is emphasizing the anointing that was upon Mary of Bethany, which is the anointing to "waste" our lives on one thing: extravagant devotion to Jesus Christ. It is the anointing to linger long with an engaged spirit in the presence of the Lord.[3]

Noninitiates will wonder what all the fuss is about. Like Martha, they will wonder why their sister sits while they work. But the rapt and rumpled worshippers in Spirit will not be deterred. They have discovered the secret to a passionate appetite—it is excessive devotion at the feet of the Master. They want to be captured by Him, pulled into the depths of His being—and hopefully drag some other poor and unsuspecting soul with them into the irresistible love of the Father.

COMPREHENDING OR APPREHENDING?

The John 3:16 of the Old Testament is Deuteronomy 6:4. It is
called the *Shema* of Israel. The word *shema* means "hear." It is
a call, a summons to listen to Moses's law concerning the covenant to the Jews. It goes like this: "Hear [*shema*] O Israel: The
LORD our God, the LORD is one" (Deut. 6:4). Let's stop right
there. Notice the "oneness" of our God. This is more than just
numerical oneness. It is categorical oneness. Uniqueness. It is
similar to the idea of holiness. When we say that God is one
or that He is holy, we mean that He is "other." That is, there is
nothing else in all creation like Him. As to His nature, He is
entirely "other." Jesus stated to the Samaritan woman that God
is "Spirit," meaning He's not like you and He can't be tethered to
your shrine. He's something else—literally.

This is why the Jews were forbidden to make a graven image
of Him (Exod. 20). It's not because God doesn't like beautiful
symbolism or imagery. In fact, the entire tabernacle and temple
cult was rich with ancient symbolism. The reason God would not
tolerate them making an image of Him is because there isn't an
image in all creation that would suffice. There is no analogy for
God that will do the trick. Since He existed before time and He
transcends the physical world, there is nothing in the physical
world that can quite capture Him. The "LORD our God" is one.
He is Spirit. And He is other.

This means that there are aspects of His nature that we cannot
comprehend. Theologians refer to this as the "non-communicable"
nature of God, meaning that some of God's attributes cannot be
passed on to us. Many of His character traits do transfer: His
compassion, His communal nature, His empathy, authority,
morality, and self-awareness. All of these traits He has passed on
to us. But there are mysterious aspects of His nature that we will
never understand, like His trinitarian nature, His infinite nature,
or even His sovereign choices. I don't get how He can be omni-
scient (all-knowing), omnipotent (all-powerful), or omnipresent

(everywhere at once). As finite beings, we will never quite comprehend these enigmatic aspects of His nature. Does this mean that God is off-limits to us? Not at all. Just because we can't comprehend Him doesn't mean we can't apprehend Him. What do I mean by this?

By way of example, my children cannot fathom the scope of my responsibilities as a pastor, as a professor, or as a husband to their mommy. They don't understand the complexities of the homework I grade, and they don't understand all the protocol and details of my daily existence interacting in professional environments. For that matter, they don't even know how to order my favorite beverage: a 16-ounce, nonfat, two-pump almond latte with a pinch of cinnamon (I know, I'm one of those annoying people).

Though my kids don't *comprehend* all the complexities of my life and responsibilities, they can, however, *apprehend*, or experience me, as their dad. When I get down on the floor with them to wrestle and toss them around, or squeeze and snuggle them, I am real and their experience of me is real. They can tussle with me, jump on my back, and roll around on the floor. I can also bring my knowledge down to their shelf. I can help them with their homework, or explain a Bible story, or teach them how to build a model car. I may not be able to explain all of the densities of my adult existence, like balancing a checkbook or paying taxes, but they can encounter the essence of me in their little worlds.

You see, you don't have to have a full explanation of something to experience its fullness of essence. And this is true with the Spirit of God. He is *other*. Meaning, we will never fathom some aspects of His wisdom and His nature. Yet we can love Him deeply from the heart. Listen to how Moses put it: "You shall love the LORD your God with all your heart and with all your soul and with all your might" (Deut. 6:5, ESV). It turns out that Israel failed to live up to this love decree—not because they didn't want to, and not because God wasn't lovable. It's because they didn't have the Spirit of God poured out into their hearts yet. The decree had been established to show that it couldn't be followed without the Spirit's power. They had the decree but no presence—no Daddy on the floor ready to consume them with His Spirit and love. They were members of a fallen race and lost in their sins because they didn't have the gift of the Spirit to transform them.

Mow Their Lawn as You Would Mow Your Own

The Jews in Jesus's day would recite the *Shema* four times a day, and I'm sure Jesus did too. The disciples relentlessly worked this creed into their teachings, and the earliest Christian communities practiced the Jesus creed as the centerpiece of their Christian worship.[4] When Jesus was questioned about the greatest command, He turned the issue back to the questioner. "How do you see it?" Jesus asked. The questioner recited the *Shema*. And Jesus commended him. He then stated that the second command was like it: "Love your neighbor as yourself." Love for God should always result in a concern for those made in His image. It is an extension of our heavenward love.

My neighbor, a young teacher in her late thirties, passed away a couple of years ago. I came home one day to revolving red and blue lights in front of her house. The officers met me on the sidewalk and told me that she had died from complications of the H1N1 virus. Her family found her in her bed. She died in her sleep.

Well, they might as well have Tasered me. I stood there in shock, thinking of all our recent interactions with her. Just a few days earlier we had tried to deliver the candy she'd ordered from my boys. My kids would often see her dogs and run out to catch them and play with them. Now Lacey, that was her name, was gone. Just like that.

I fought back the tears while the officers filled me in on how she'd been found.

Then, very quietly, bag in hand, I snuck into the front door of my house. It was warm in my house. My children were all up in the kitchen laughing and drawing pictures, and my wife was cooking dinner. On any given night you can walk into my house around 5:30 p.m. and hear the percussion of "happy noise." I felt as if I'd walked out of a nightmare into a dream. I stood there in my doorway still stunned by the news.

All night, I couldn't stop thinking about Lacey's passing. How had she faced her last moments? Was she ready?

I felt convicted by the Spirit. I used to frequently bellyache that she hardly ever weeded and mowed her lawn. I'd mumble under my breath how I wished her brother, who lived with her, would trim that unkempt yard full of weeds. But I realized it had never occurred to me once to mow her lawn or help her weed it.

I also groused every winter when we had snow. I'd go to the mailbox thinking, "Why doesn't Lacey ever shovel her snow?" I am ashamed to admit that I rarely, if ever, used my snow blower to remove the snow from her walkway. I thought I was a great neighbor until she was gone. Then I started thinking back, "Had she ever dropped a hint or floated the idea of needing help in any of our curbside conversations? Why didn't I listen? What made me think I was such a great neighbor in the first place?" Perhaps I couldn't hear her over the sound of my own awesomeness. But I had missed my opportunity to be the living gospel—and now she was gone.

When you read Jesus's words, "Love your neighbor as you love yourself," do you just tune it out—does it just sound like religious static because you've heard a thousand sermons on it? For the rest of my life, I will hear that verse this way: "Mow your neighbor's lawn, as you would mow your own."

This experience changed me. I began to be a better neighbor. A couple of years later Lacey's empty home was finally bought by a young couple. They moved their stuff in, and I walked over and offered to help them with their lawn. I walked the young man over to my garage and showed him my weak collection of tools and offered to let him borrow anything he needed. I invited him and his wife over for dinner. I even weeded his yard when he wasn't home. I had been converted in a most practical way. Paul's litany to the Corinthians on love's virtues isn't in the abstract for me anymore:

- Love is relentless—it won't give up.
- Love is self-less—it thinks of others.
- Love doesn't crave what it doesn't have.
- It doesn't strut or swagger.
- It doesn't vaunt itself as something special.
- It isn't aggressive and bellicose—it is easygoing.
- Love doesn't come unhinged when others are in the wrong.
- It doesn't tally the sins of fellow believers.
- It doesn't revel in the failure of rivals.
- Love celebrates the truth, tolerates the intolerable, trusts when hope seems lost, assumes the best in people, and endures with unflinching commitment—right to the bitter end. Love cannot fail (1 Cor. 13:4–8).

Loving God and loving people is the very environment of a Spirit-empowered church. Affectionate love for the Father and selfless love for others is the key to unleashing the power of the Spirit and the power of the gospel in our lives.

Paul wanted the New Testament church to be a community marked by selfless love for others, a community that reached out to those suffering in the self-made hell of addictions, ignorance, and shame. He wanted those gifted people to excel at the one thing that will never pass away—it will never cease—because it is the character and quality of God Himself: love. Love never fails. God is love. And God "has poured out his love into our hearts by the Holy Spirit" (Rom. 5:5). The Spirit makes it possible for us to receive and to be carriers of this holy contagion—God's love. When He is poured out into our hearts, we become Spirit-gifted love machines.

PART THREE
EMBRACE THE MYSTERY
How do I embrace life in the Spirit today?

WHILE TYPING AWAY on this book one evening, I noticed a little red light kept popping up in my peripheral vision. Like a crazy man, I spent the next hour trying to trap it or dart my eyes sideways to re-create it. I even googled mental conditions that caused one to see red lights in their peripheral vision and contemplated making a doctor's appointment for it. Turns out, it was just the reflection of my mouse sensor off a shiny book on my desk.

Have you ever seen something that wasn't really there? Fear is a powerful motivator. Fear can create entire worlds in the mind that do not actually exist—and yet we act as if they do.

Now, there are some healthy kinds of fear that we need if we are going to survive in the world and thrive as Jesus's disciples. We need the rational fear that can trigger our sympathetic nervous systems to either bolt or be bold in the face of danger. We also need to live with a healthy fear of God—and by that I do not mean "reverent awe" or some other tepid euphemism for godly fear. There is a wondrous dread, or a glorious sense of panic that God's presence brings, and it is *healthy fear*. Brennan Manning described God as "an awesome, incomprehensible, and unwieldy Mystery."[1] This God is an all-consuming fire, and raging fires should be handled with the utmost care.

But there is an irrational fear that is destructive to our discipleship. It's the fear that causes us to reorder our lives on the basis of groundless possibilities. It's the fear I walk around with for several days after watching every episode of Discovery Channel's "Shark Week" with my boys. Now, I don't live anywhere near the coast, and I haven't been swimming in the ocean for years—but I'm deathly afraid of getting eaten by a ravenous great white. That's just an irrational fear that has little to do with my reality. But the mind is easily duped. People are afraid of all kinds of things today:

- Ablutophobia—fear of bathing (I think my kids have this)

- Hippopoto/monstrous/equippe/dalio/phobia— fear of big words

- Phobophobia—fear of acquiring a new fear

- Panphobia—fear of everything!

These kinds of fears, though real, are silly in the extreme. Yet many of us struggle with unfounded fear that keeps us from living in the fullness of God's presence. I call this *pneuma-phobia*—fear of the Spirit. We're concerned that if we embrace this mysterious life in the Spirit, we might get labeled a "charismaniac" or wind up bingeing on emotionalism. But let us not excuse a dry and empty Christian life simply because we are afraid of extremism. I have news for you: if you've been born again into Jesus's kingdom, you're already a fanatic.

Weirdo.

Oddball.

Freak.

Christian. And so you might as well go all the way and embrace the awesome power of the Spirit.

Part 3 of this book will encourage us to step out in faith. A comfort zone, by definition, is an anxiety-neutral space where we are never challenged and we avoid anything that may be "unsafe." But God never intended the Christian life to be anxiety-neutral. We need all of the resources of heaven to meet the challenges of the valley of the shadow of death. (See Psalm 23.) We need to embrace His baptism, live filled with His presence, and replace carnal desires with His desires as we punch up our commitment on spiritual disciplines. Lastly, we need to act according to the value system of the kingdom age in the power of the Spirit. All of this takes faith. Living in the Spirit's presence requires risk.

12

BUILT TO HOLD FIRE

Embrace the Spirit's fire.

How else do you explain the inexplicable, except in
a rush of images from the world we already know?[1]
—N. T. WRIGHT—

WHEN I WAS a kid, I was a bit of pyro. I would steal the
wood stove matches my dad thought he'd hidden in
the cabinet, and I'd go deep into the woods behind our house
to experiment with them. Only on occasion did a fire get a bit
out of control, which is how my brother and I burned my dad's
workshop down. But burning Dad's old wooden shed down was
nothing compared to what I did one Sunday morning.

Just before leaving for church, I decided to light a small fire—
just a quick one. I didn't have time to go very far into the woods,
so I stayed close to my house. Later that morning in church the
pastor honored our local firefighters for their service. My mother
could not have anticipated that the very firefighters standing in
the church sanctuary that morning would later be putting out a
burning hell in our backyard!

That's the last fire I ever set.

I'll never forget the look of fear on my dad's face while
standing in our driveway. That fire really shook him, and I could
see it. The expression of fear on his face was more powerful than
any spanking I could have ever gotten. And besides, there was

literally no woodshed for him to take me out to anyway because by now it was a pile of charred scree.

Fire is an interesting thing. Fire can warm you on a cold night. It can light your way and guide your steps. Fire can be converted to energy and start your car so you can get to work in the morning. And if you think for one minute you can do without fire, just try to go a month without using any electricity. Did you know that the majority of electricity usage in America comes from burning fossil fuels?[2] There are so many good uses of fire, and we couldn't get along without it.

But fire can also be responsible for untold devastation. The same fire that warms you can kill you. And many of us know someone who has personally experienced the wreckage of a house fire. Among the charred items and blackened rubble, usually only the chimney or wood stove is left standing. As my friend Steve likes to say, it's because chimneys were built to hold fire.

In the same way, you and I were built to hold the Spirit's fire. Jesus wants to cast a purifying fire on you—a baptism of the Spirit—an empowering presence that will consume you and enable you to do the impossible.

THE VOICE

The Scriptures portray John the Baptist as a fiery sage, preaching and prophesying in northern Israel. The region where John preached was a hotbed for messianic uprisings. Years earlier men like Judas the Galilean led a revolt against Rome. This revolution resulted in many Jewish men—husbands, fathers, sons—dying horrible deaths by crucifixion.[3] The area where John preached was the source for these types of rebellions in the name of the messiah. No doubt John's ministry style would have garnered considerable attention from those with an appetite for revolution—especially those who were looking for the next "messiah." But he would also have gotten the attention of those who were a bit jumpy and apprehensive at the thought of another messianic dissident.

Calling John "the Baptist" had a particular meaning for his audience. In his day there were essentially two types of baptisms: ritual purity immersion and proselyte baptism. Ritual purity immersion was a common, everyday experience. It was thought by the Jews that these ritual cleansings were rooted in their Hebrew Bible. It was also thought that they were efficacious—meaning, the Jews believed these ritual cleansings really did keep them pure in God's sight from the typical contaminants of bodily discharges, poor complexion, menstrual cycles, and contacting dead bodies, which was common due to the mortality rate in the ancient world.

But it appears that John did not adopt the run-of-the-mill ritual purity cleansing method. Instead he appeared to be calling the nation of Israel to repentance and to receive a proselyte baptism (Luke 3:3). This would have been very unusual. Proselyte or evangelistic baptism was reserved for the Gentiles who were out of covenant with Yahweh, the Hebrew God.[4] John was calling people to a baptism of *repentance*. Jews did not practice repentance baptism because, in their view, they had nothing to repent of. They were God's chosen people, they had Abraham as their father, they studied and read the Torah, they attended the national feasts, they ate a kosher diet, and they met in the synagogue on the Sabbath. From what would they repent? Yet the text says they came out to John confessing their sins.

Though they may have thought of themselves as insiders, John's shocking message to these Torah-observant Jews was that they were, like the unsavory Gentiles, outsiders.[5] They needed the washing and baptism of repentance. This is why John's message challenging their Abrahamic pedigree was so jarring and raised some eyebrows:

> Produce fruit in keeping with repentance. And do not begin to say to yourselves, "We have Abraham as our father." For I tell you that out of these stones God can raise up children for Abraham. The ax is already at the

root of the trees, and every tree that does not produce good fruit will be cut down and thrown into the fire.

—LUKE 3:8–9

When the leaders of Israel show up to cross-examine John's preaching and methods, they want to know:

+ Is he the Messiah or the prophet?

and...

+ If he is not the Messiah or the prophet, then by whose authority is he performing repentance baptisms on observant Jews? (See John 1:19–28.)

John's response was cryptic: "I am the voice." John's answer means that he viewed himself—his very own identity—to be swallowed up in his mission. The leaders of John's day were hung up on the pomp and tinsel of their honorific titles. John answered by saying, "I won't be joining your elitist club." Instead his response was, "My title is my message—my message is who I am—the voice of one crying out in arid places—get ready, get ready because everything is going to change." How would it change?

John continued:

> I baptize you with water. But one more powerful than I will come....He will baptize you with the Holy Spirit and fire. His winnowing fork is in his hand to clear his threshing floor and to gather the wheat into his barn, but he will burn up the chaff with unquenchable fire.
>
> —LUKE 3:16–17

What was John talking about with all this "unquenchable fire" language?

IT'S A NEW DAWN; IT'S A NEW DAY

When the true Messiah comes, said John, He would immerse them in God's presence—a presence that was like a purifying fire. This heavenly downpour of the Spirit would result in repentant humanity being reinstated to the Father's house, partaking of His divine life again. The outcome of this event is humanity's entrance into the new era—the messianic age of the Spirit.

What's surprising about all this is that John had to baptize *Jesus Himself* to complete God's righteous plan. John was perplexed that Jesus showed up for a proselyte baptism. Surely the Christ did not need to repent. Surely the pure Lamb of God who takes away the world's sins should baptize John instead. But Jesus's response to the flummoxed Baptist was "Let it be so now; it is proper for us to do this to fulfill all righteousness" (Matt. 3:15). What specifically about His baptism fulfilled God's righteous plan?

Jesus's own baptism in water and Spirit signified His personal entrance into the new epoch, the messianic age.[6] Jesus is often spoken of as "the firstfruits" of this new humanity who will be transformed by the Spirit (1 Cor. 15:20). This is why Paul calls Him the "*firstborn* among many brothers" (Rom. 8:29, emphasis added) and the "*firstborn* from among the dead" (Col. 1:18, emphasis added). Jesus's baptism did more than inaugurate His earthly ministry. It initiated the new kingdom age whereby God was restoring His presence to lost men. This baptism of Spirit and fire introduced them to a new era—the new covenant. At the coming of the Messiah, the Spirit would be poured out onto all flesh. But this outpouring could not take place until Jesus experienced another baptism. It is the baptism by fire.

A STRESSED-OUT MESSIAH

Now that the Messiah had come and the kingdom had broken into our fallen world, only one thing stopped people from experiencing this kingdom life by the Spirit: purity of heart. Adam and Eve's sin didn't just put a wrinkle in our rapport with the Almighty. It was a devastating loss of life—the Spirit's life in us (Eph. 2:1). The result was that humankind faced inner death or separation from God. That separation was due to the impurity of heart through rebellion.

Glancing at the Genesis story, one might conclude that God is a persnickety deity whose feathers are easily ruffled over minor stuff like eating fruit from the wrong tree. Seems kind of nitpicky doesn't it? Yet nothing could be farther from the truth. Instead, the garden story in Genesis shows us that the smallest infraction of God's commands, like the eating of forbidden fruit, is an affront to the infinite holiness of our God. Sampling the garden contraband was a gateway sin. And we have rushed farther and farther out of His presence ever since.

The only thing left for Jesus to do for mankind was to drink the cup of God's wrath (Luke 22:42)—to undergo the baptism of fire and judgment through a vicarious, substitutionary death on a cross. This baptism of fire is what was needed to bring mankind back to the garden of God's restored presence. Jesus's Spirit baptism allowed *Him* to participate in the new age of the Spirit. But in order for *everyone else* to partake, He had to finish His baptism. This is why Jesus cryptically stated, "I came to cast fire on the earth, and would that it were already kindled! I have a baptism to be baptized with, and how great is my distress until it is accomplished!" (Luke 12:49–50, ESV). Jesus was anxious to start the process of "casting fire" on the earth. Jesus is the representative and the servant of lost humanity who completes His work by receiving the full brunt of God's judgment.[7]

The part of Jesus's statement that is most surprising to me is "how great is my distress" (v. 50, ESV). I don't typically picture Jesus as being stressed out. Why was Jesus distressed until that baptism of fire had been poured out on Him?

He was distressed by empty religion.

I firmly believe that Jesus experienced great anguish by watching His fellow countrymen get it all wrong—or at least most of it. The Pharisees, or the *perushim* (separate ones), thought the way to God was through diligent and exacting religion. Jesus scolded them for erecting a meritocracy—a system based on merit and performance. Theirs was a practiced devotion that never really went beyond yammering lips (Matt. 23).

Then there were the Sadducees, or the *zadakoi* (priestly ones). The Sadducees lived to feather their own nests and, like the Pharisees, cared little for the rabble in Galilee.[8] These men were compromisers and elitists. They rejected most of the Hebrew Bible and weren't particularly excited about God's kingdom coming to earth to right wrongs and overturn inequities.

Another party was the Zealots, or *zelotes* (passionate ones). The Zealot faction thought the way to God's heart was to subvert the Roman Empire through military uprisings. Jesus utterly rejected this approach and instead told them to turn the other cheek and go the extra mile. God's kingdom would not come as a result of military incursion or revolution. Their path led to Rome's slaughter of many of Jesus's countrymen, and this surely caused Jesus angst.

Conversely, the Essenes thought that Jews should withdraw from the world and live in a compound to impress God with their asceticism. Jesus had no appetite at all for withdrawing from the world into a holy commune. He wanted His disciples to be in the world but not of it.

Jesus seemed stressed out by these false Judaisms. No one was advancing closer to God in these bogus systems of Jewish religion. Every now and then Jesus experienced a holy flare-up on wrongheaded religion (Matt. 23). He knew that only the Spirit's restored presence could reinstate lost humanity and unwind the injustices and inequities of our fallen world.

He was distressed by the effects of sin.

Jesus was also distressed over people in the grip of sin. He came to free them from slavery to their lusts and their idolatries. Jesus stated, "Everyone who sins is a slave to sin" (John 8:34). He came to equip His fellow Jews to live in the fruit of the Spirit, something the law could never do for them (Rom. 7:6). And He came to offer the Greek pagans another shot at life by giving them access to the God of the Hebrews. The people living in darkness have seen an irresistible light—a light that would lead them away from their worthless idols and back to the Father's house. The way was transformation by the Spirit.

He was distressed by injustice.

Jesus was also distraught over the injustices and inequities of society. The wealthy inherited riches and the poor had little opportunity for upward mobility. In His day you stayed in the station in life where you were born. The materially wealthy and the spiritually rich were usually the same group of people. Their wealth meant that they could afford the finest rabbinic education in the Torah. But Jesus came for the poor and the poor in spirit. He came for the disadvantaged and disenfranchised masses. He came to mend sick people back to health and to restore men to paradise—back to life in the Spirit.

Jesus came to save us from all that is wrong with our existence. This happens partially now and fully later in our resurrection. But before He could dispense the Spirit to humanity, casting a purifying fire onto the earth, before He could restore all flesh to relationship with their heavenly Father—He had to undergo a horrific baptism of fire Himself. It was a cleansing fire that would give mankind access to the God who dwells in unapproachable light.

But how do you purify a Savior who is without sin?

That Savior must take onto Himself the sins of a lost race. That Messiah, bearing the sins of humanity, must be the focal point of God's wrath and His cross must be the bridge between heaven and earth—between the realm of light and the realm of darkness. Jesus's statement "How I wish [that fire] were already kindled!" (Luke 12:49) takes on new meaning now that we understand that the Spirit's presence in our lives is a purifying fire that reinstates us by burning off the "chaff" of sin that separates us from our Father. This is made possible because Jesus suffered on the cross and bore the impact of God's wrath.

THE SOLEMN PACT

No wonder Jesus was anxious to send the disciples the Spirit. Yet nothing could have been further from the disciples' expectations. They embraced the widely held view that when the Messiah came, He would exact His vengeance on the nations. They thought the gospel meant that their pagan oppressors were finally getting what was coming to them. Their view was almost entirely nationalistic, and they had no concept of the baptism of fire and Spirit that they needed to undergo. Though they believed in a bodily resurrection at the end of the old age to start the new kingdom age for Jews, they couldn't fathom Jesus's message about a reborn humanity or a spiritually reconstituted human race.

Before Jesus was taken into the heavenly realms, He reassured the disciples that He would send them this promise of the Father—the baptism of the Spirit and fire (Acts 1:8). This was a solemn pact, a take-it-to-the-bank kind of thing. On Pentecost, this is just what took place. The Spirit that Jesus had received was now being unleashed on a faithful community—and that community would be the catalyst for God pouring out His Spirit on all flesh.

A HOLY WRECKING

The process of entering Jesus's kingdom, entering this new messianic age of the Spirit, is one of becoming utterly undone so that we may be completely remade. This is what Spirit baptism is all about. The baptizer is Jesus—the firstfruits of Spirit baptism.

We have faith in His baptism of fire on the cross and His resurrection from the dead, and we receive the Spirit, which involves a winnowing fork. John the Baptist used this image to illustrate what the Savior would do for the people of God. This winnowing fork is for the purpose of separating the wheat from the chaff, the faithful from the faithless.

Separation is always a metaphor for purity in Scripture. Then, the Spirit ignites the chaff and burns it away, leaving a purified crop. This process of Spirit baptism is how we gain entrance into the kingdom of God, just as Jesus entered the end of the age at His baptism,[9] and it is also the source of our continued renewal and empowerment for life in that new age of the Spirit. Immersion in the Spirit's presence is both simultaneous to our conversion and the subsequent experience of the redeemed (more on that in the next chapter).

CHURCH, WIND, AND FIRE

Scholar N. T. Wright beautifully describes the scene at Pentecost:

> I want you to imagine for a moment that you have just thrown open the window on a glorious spring morning. A fresh breeze is stirring around the garden. In the distance there is a crackle of bonfire as a farmer clears away some winter rubbish. Out in the field, a skylark is hovering over its nest. All around, there is a sense of creation throwing off its wintry coverings and getting ready for an outburst of new life.
>
> All these are images the early Christians used to describe something strange but real and central to their lives. They spoke of a powerful wind rushing through the house and entering them. They spoke of tongues of fire resting on them and transforming them. They picked up, from the ancient creation story, the image of a bird brooding over the waters of chaos to bring order and life to birth.[10]

On the Day of Pentecost the believers were all together, faithfully waiting for Jesus's promise of renewal (Acts 2:1). As they waited, from out of nowhere, or perhaps everywhere, the Spirit of God was poured out in their midst. Several signs accompanied this experience. Let's put these signs into perspective for our day.

First, there was a sound like a gale force wind.

Scripture states that they heard what sounded like a "Spirit storm," or violent gusts of wind/breath. The Greek word for "wind" or "breath" is *pnoe*, which means "breath of life." This surely draws on Ezekiel's valley of dry bones vision (Ezek. 37:9–14).[11] In this vision Ezekiel sees a valley full of dead men's bones, which symbolizes Israel dead in their sins. Ezekiel calls to the wind, and the Spirit of God comes and the breath of God reconstitutes their dead bones.

Jesus used this same analogy when He stated to Nicodemus, "The wind blows where it wishes, and you hear its sound, but you do not know where it comes from or where it goes. So it is with everyone who is born of the Spirit" (John 3:8, esv). Remember, Adam was made a living being when God breathed life into his nostrils. Mankind lost the presence of God in the garden through spiritual death. John Levison notes, "The opening scene of the human drama, though set amidst a garden of delight, echoes against the implacable cliffs of the valley of the shadow of death."[12] The result was our loss of the "vitality of divine inbreathing."[13] The same divine "face" intimately pressed against ours, breathing into our nostrils, now turns away from us and is hidden, taking away the Spirit (Gen. 3:8). The loss of the Spirit's life—separation from the Father—resulted in our expulsion from paradise and being plunged into a state of death. The first thing that was restored at Pentecost was the Spirit's life to the spiritually dead. The bones are reanimated—the people of God are reconstituted as the "breath," or wind, of God once again blows through the community of faith. Bringing life. Bringing power.

Second, there was the distribution of fiery tongues.

And there appeared to them fire tongues that distributed and rested on each one of them. "And they were all filled with the Holy Spirit and began to speak in other tongues as the Spirit gave them utterance" (Acts 2:4, ESV). Why would speaking in other languages be the sign of the Spirit's return to lost humanity? Many have noted that ecstatic speech forms usually followed God's fiery self-revelations (Exod. 19:18; 2 Sam. 22:16; Ezek. 13:13).[14] But that observation is perhaps too zoomed in. I am convinced that this is but an echo of the real significance for this sign at Pentecost.

The Book of Genesis contains a series of judgments that are a result of the fall of Adam and Eve. One of the more striking judgments is the dispersion of people in the land of Shinar (Gen. 11:2). Moses describes the scene as one of social and linguistic unity. Yet evil had taken deep root in these people's hearts, for they desired to be gods. The text says they sought to "make a name" for themselves (v. 4). This is pagan code for "sought to achieve immortality."[15]

God judged these settlers in Shinar for essentially trying to build a ziggurat tall enough to reach the dome or the sky that they thought was in reach just above them—what is referred to as the Tower of Babel. God had no problem with human ingenuity or unity. But the unified pursuit of the wrong thing can lead to tragic consequences and fearful enterprises.[16] So He scattered them and brought confusion to the *lingua franca*—the language of commerce they all had in common.[17] God's judgment is clearly characterized by *fracturing corrupt unity*. God intended to shatter their evil pursuit of immortality by breaking up their culture through diverse languages.

So at Pentecost we have a beautiful picture of fractured humanity being restored. The disciples' ability to speak unlearned languages, or for that matter heavenly speech, was a sign to the crowd that the Spirit was restored in a newly constituted humanity. The losses of Eden are paid back with interest. This is why there is such an emphasis on Christian unity in the New Testament and almost no emphasis on it prior to Pentecost—because the Spirit makes it possible to do something we could never do while we were in our sin: live in unity. Paul wrote to the Ephesians:

> Make every effort to keep the unity of the Spirit through the bond of peace. There is one body and one Spirit—just as you were called to one hope when you were called—one Lord, one faith, one baptism; one God and Father of all, who is over all and through all and in all.
> —EPHESIANS 4:3–6

Likewise Paul encourages the Christians to be of one mind and one voice so that they may bring glory to God (Rom. 15:5–6; 2 Cor. 13:11; Phil. 2:2). This fulfills Jesus's prayer for the disciples' complete unity (John 17:23). The restored presence of God restores our lost vocation—*one family worshipping one God under heaven.*

Though Paul will explain to the Corinthians later that speaking in tongues can be a powerful mode of private or corporate prayer (1 Cor. 14:2, 4, 14), in the Acts 2 passage its primary purpose is as a sign to the scattered nations that the Spirit has been restored and the division that was part of the curse is now unwound. God is now coalescing people from all nations back into one family, and that family—though we are ethnically and socially and linguistically diverse—now speaks the "language" of the Spirit. Though not every believer can speak unlearned languages per se, we all have the Spirit to which the sign pointed. God's ideal for community is found in the church when it is functioning as He intended. Notice the table of nations in Acts 2:5–11. The first place we see this table of nations list is in Genesis 10, right before the judgment in Shinar at the tower construction site. Of these scattered nations, God says through the prophet Isaiah:

> And I, because of their actions and their imaginations, am about to come and gather all nations and tongues, and they will come and see my glory. I will set a sign among them, and I will send some of those who survive to the nations—to Tarshish, to the Libyans and Lydians (famous as archers), to Tubal and Greece, and to the distant islands that have not heard of my fame or seen my glory. They will proclaim my glory among the nations. And they will bring all your brothers, from all the nations, to my holy mountain in Jerusalem as an offering to the LORD.
>
> —ISAIAH 66:18–20

The Isaiah passage states three things about the nations: 1) that God would gather the people from among the nations to "see" His glory; 2) that God would send a remnant of Jews to all nations and languages; and 3) the result of proclaiming God's glory among the nations was to bring all of them to His "holy mountain" as an offering. That is, the purpose of God gathering these remnant Jews was to show them a sign of His presence and then send them back out to the nations to evangelize the peoples of the earth. This is precisely what we see take place in Acts. And this is why Jesus told His followers to go and make disciples of all the nations (Matt. 28:19–20). The gospel is an announcement that through Jesus and baptism in the Spirit we can now rejoin the family of God. All of humanity can be restored!

And notice the utter confusion of the crowds on the Day of Pentecost. This confusion is by design. Whenever the Spirit does something in our midst, our first response is usually bewilderment. But if we will stick around long enough for the explanation, we may find ourselves in the middle of a miracle. The Jews at Pentecost couldn't read the situation, so they begin to fill in the blanks. "Maybe these Jews are drunk? Perhaps the celebration has gotten the best of them? Maybe they've cracked?" But confusion can be the prelude to acuity. Don't be too quick to bail on a murky season in your life. Clarity can punch through the fog when you least expect it. The miracle of restored sight has only one prerequisite: *blindness.*

Transparency is the real enigma. It is the illusion of intelligibility. This is why humanity spends every waking moment disagreeing about everything under the sun. Our very language is cursed—we are doomed to be fractured by it. Only the Spirit can bring estranged mankind back into relationship. Language can heal, but only when it is the Spirit's language—what Paul referred to as "words taught to us by the Spirit." It is the vernacular of the kingdom age.

So don't be offended by God using a variety of tongues as a sign of Him coalescing the nations—He's just unwinding a curse that began in Genesis.

Third, the Spirit was available to all.

Peter interprets the Pentecost outpouring to a confused crowd. He quotes the prophet Joel regarding the Spirit being poured out on everyone.

> "'In the last days, God says, I will pour out my Spirit on all people. Your sons and daughters will prophesy, your young men will see visions, your old men will dream dreams. Even on my servants, both men and women, I will pour out my Spirit in those days, and they will prophesy....' Exalted to the right hand of God, he has received from the Father the promised Holy Spirit and has poured out what you now see and hear...." Peter replied, "Repent and be baptized, every one of you, in the name of Jesus Christ for the forgiveness of your sins. And you will receive the gift of the Holy Spirit. The promise is for you and your children and for all who are far off—for all whom the Lord our God will call."
>
> —Acts 2:17–18, 33, 38–39

Peter understands this language in Joel as being the outpouring of the Holy Spirit in various abilities and on all walks of life: men, women, children, people of all ages. The Spirit was restored. Jesus had cast fire to the earth, and now those who repent—all who repent—can receive the Spirit by faith. The distinguishing mark of this new community is that they are a fellowship of prophets, all walks of life speaking the words taught them by the Spirit.

The Spirit is for you, for your children, and for all generations. All men and women can be a part of Jesus's new humanity. It starts with baptism—with a purifying fire, baptism in power, and personal transformation. God wants to fix that which was broken. He wants to heal that which was sick. He wants to gather the scattered nations into this messianic family.

WHERE NO JEW HAS GONE BEFORE

Fourth, the Spirit empowered them for the impossible.

The Spirit's presence isn't just to restore lost humanity back to relationship with the Father. He baptizes us that we may receive power—the divine enabling to do the impossible.

Just think for a moment how impossible the church's situation was. Their Savior had been crucified and risen, and then left them again—by themselves—or so they thought. The authority structures in Jerusalem had already shown their intolerance for dissident viewpoints. The Roman government did not allow new cults, and it required citizens to pledge their allegiance to Caesar, who was thought to be a god. Caesar's "gospel" of peace and Roman might permeated every town and municipality—every crack and crevice of Roman life. A message about a risen rabbi who proclaimed Himself the vindicated Lord of the universe would not go over well in the power structures into which the church was about to be launched.

One day before they are baptized in Spirit and fire—they cower behind closed doors in a rented flat. One day after they are baptized in Spirit and fire—they boldly go where no Jew has gone before. Their transformation was experiential, phenomenological, and irrepressible. Nothing could stop them from the mission.

Not the Sanhedrin.

Not Caesar.

Not death itself.

They became men and women on fire. And I want to live in that fire—to be cleansed and shaped and propelled outward by it.

BUILT FOR IT

In the next few chapters we are going to explore what it means to live in the flame. Fire is purifying, but it is also catalytic. An untended fire will burn out—or burn *out of control*. But a well-tended fire will produce all kinds of good stuff in our lives. The choice is ours. We can choose to be moved to action, kindling and stoking the fires of worship, self-discipline, desire for God, pure living, and faith. Or we can allow our fire to burn out as we languish in a Spirit-deprived existence. Now that we have been remade, baptized in the Spirit, and cleansed in the fire of Jesus's sufferings, we need to live in the flame empowered to *be His witnesses*.

13

UNDER THE INFLUENCE
Embrace Spirit-filled living.

> O Holy Spirit...descend plentifully into my
> heart! Lighten the dark corners of this neglected
> dwelling and scatter there thy cheerful beams![1]
> —AUGUSTINE—

I THINK SHE MUST have been about fourteen years old. And she was completely oblivious to her surroundings. The teenage girl was walking down the beach, lagging behind her mother and little brothers while texting on her smartphone.

A vacation to the Oregon Coast just reassures you that there must be a God—the soothing rhythm of the breakers, the texture of fine sand between your toes as you soak and soften in warm sunrays on a mid-August day. Then there are the cyclopean boulders jutting out of the water. Not to mention the miles of shoreline and the verdant mountain valleys and the camel-colored dunes...

So as a lazy worshipper sitting in my beach chair, I was struck at the sight of a young girl texting her BFF while unconscious to the beauty all around her.

Suddenly, out of nowhere, a wave snuck up and crashed over the young girl. Her mom and brothers burst out laughing, chortling as she stood there drenched—phone soaked and hair flattened. Then, to her credit, she put away the cell phone and began to splash around and they all laughed and played for a bit. In the same way sometimes we encounter those surprising moments when God's Spirit seems to crash into our distracted worlds to remind us why we're on this planet.

God put us on this earth so that we might revel in His glory as we consider the sprawling grandeur of His creation. We were made to commune with God's Spirit as we inhale the salty fumes of ocean water crashing white at our feet. We rediscover our God-given purpose every time we encounter a stunning vista or the contagious giggling of a happy baby. Subconsciously we reason that if the *effect* is this awesome, then just imagine what the *cause* must be like. Sensing God's presence in His handiwork should naturally stimulate us to worship. And that's not by accident. Before mankind sinned in the garden, we enjoyed immediate access to God's presence.

Now in faith, God has reestablished relationship with us, and we are reinstated as His sons and daughters. This "plentiful descent" that Augustine spoke of is what Paul referred to as being "filled with the Spirit." Being filled with God's Spirit is the ongoing experience of the Christian life. And it can happen anywhere at any time. But it is amplified as we give voice to our passion for the heavenly Father.[2]

BEHAVIORAL OR EXPERIENTIAL?

Paul told the Ephesian Christians that experiencing the Spirit as a transforming reality ought to be a regular occurrence in the Christian life.

> Therefore do not be foolish, but understand what the Lord's will is. Do not get drunk on wine, which leads to debauchery. Instead, be filled with the Spirit. Speak to one another with psalms, hymns and spiritual songs. Sing and make music from your heart to the Lord, always giving thanks to God the Father for everything,

in the name of our Lord Jesus Christ. Submit to one
another out of reverence for Christ.
—EPHESIANS 5:17–21

Some writers and theologians incorrectly view being *filled* with
the Spirit as a synonym for the Spirit's *control*.[3] This interpretation is based on passages like Luke 4:28, which states, "All the
people in the synagogue were *furious* [*filled with rage*] when they
heard this" (emphasis added), and Acts 13:45, which says, "But
when the Jews saw the crowds, they were *filled with jealousy* and
began contradicting the things spoken by Paul" (NAS, emphasis
added). Furthermore, Paul contrasts Spirit-filling with pagan
drunkenness: "Don't be drunk on wine," he insists. It is true that
drunkenness was most commonly associated with Dionysus, the
god of wine. The worshippers of Dionysus would imbibe alcohol
until they went into an ecstatic state—claiming to lose control
as the gods possessed them.[4] So commentators look at all this
and conclude that "being filled" means "to be controlled," because
obviously these rioters and idolaters experienced a loss of self-
control to emotion or to a substance. Now, notice that none of
these passages in question actually state that the people were
controlled by their jealousy or rage or alcoholism. I maintain
that this "filling as control" theory is neither explicitly nor tacitly
present in these texts.

The problem with this "filling as control" view is that it skips
a step. These people weren't being robotically controlled by their
emotions or strong drink—*they were actually experiencing rage,
jealousy, or drunkenness.* Though emotionalism may have led
the Jews to come unhinged at Jesus or Paul—though excessive
drinking may have led to becoming possessed by an evil spirit in
pagan worship—those rioters and pagans were getting spiritually
worked up. They were eyeball-deep in their experience of it. This
is why the biblical writer describes them as being "filled" with
something.

I suspect that this "filling as control" interpretation

conveniently gets some people out of having to define Spirit filling in metaphysical terms. So the "control" view, according to some, is merely *behavioral*—that is, the Spirit mysteriously gives us the ability to rein in our passions and sinful appetites. He controls us to make sure we "behave" like good Christians. However, the use of the phrase "being filled" in the New Testament isn't primarily *behavioral*; it is *phenomenological*—that is, it is an actual experience of the Spirit that leads to greater awareness of Him in our lives.

Even when the phrase is used to describe the general character of someone like Stephen, the first church martyr, it is difficult to imagine a mere duty-driven and emotionless Stephen who was "controlled" by the Spirit. He likely would not have acquired the description of "filled with the Spirit" without a significant experiential basis for the designation. In other words, maybe Stephen was described as "full of the Holy Spirit and power" because he appeared to be awash and empowered by God's glorious presence. Sometimes it's just easier for us to crown these people with our version of Protestant sainthood—but I suspect most of us would be uncomfortable hanging around these charismaniacs were they alive and breathing today.

YOU BUY IT, YOU SEE IT

My pastor, Kurt Bubna, gives a great analogy for this. Let's say you purchase a certain model of car. Before you made the purchase, you probably only occasionally noticed that type of automobile around town. But now that you've purchased one, you start seeing cars like yours everywhere. In fact, you can't *not* see them now. The greater the experience of a thing—the greater our awareness of it.

The same is true of our lives in the Spirit. The greater your actual experience of Him, the greater your awareness of His presence and His guidance. So He doesn't fill you and mechanically take over your life, resulting in mere behavior modification.

Instead, you encounter His presence and sense Him alive in you—it is an actual spiritual phenomenon that is taking place in the depths of your being. It's as if you can't contain the experience itself—like you're going to burst at the seams with the Spirit's presence. That's why the biblical writers use synonyms like "overflowing" or "spilling over." That's the spiritual sensation. If you're going to describe the indescribable, you use the limited media of human language. So we stuff our experience of it into the limited vehicle of words.

Being filled with the Spirit means that you encounter Him to the point that He spills over and begins to influence your thoughts, passions, and choices.

Paul then gives the Ephesians the key to encountering God's Spirit this way. "Do not get drunk on wine.... Instead, be filled with the Spirit. Speak to one another with psalms, hymns and spiritual songs. Sing and make music in your heart to the Lord" (Eph. 5:18–19). In other words, replace your tavern crooning with spirited praise to the true God. Spirit-filled living was Paul's alternative to getting sloshed in the local pagan pubs. Spirit filling is a proper analogue to getting drunk because the experience of it results in coming under the influence of something, or in this case, Someone.[5]

This is why I prefer the term "influence" instead of "control." But it is influence through experience—not a mechanical control where we are mere passive instruments of some discreet and unseen work.

And worship through song is the key to unlocking this experience resulting in the Spirit's influence.

For the God Who Has Everything

I saw an interview with Bill Gates where the correspondent asked him what kind of gifts his family got him for birthdays and holidays. The implication in the question was, *What gift could Bill Gates possibly receive that he doesn't already have?* He replied that he loves getting little handmade cards and pictures from his kids. I thought, "So one of the richest billionaires in the world enjoys getting homemade crayon-scribbled cards from his children?" Objectively speaking, those cards and tokens of affection are worthless. The global equity market will not rise or fall on how well his kids scrawl pictures on construction paper. But subjectively—to Gates—those gifts have meaning because they come from the heart.

What do you get the person who has everything? This is the dilemma we face in our worship of God. Now, God knows all things and possesses all the treasures of heaven and earth. He is self-sufficient and self-sustaining and doesn't *need* anything. But there is one commodity that God longs to receive from His children. God desires for His kids to freely, boldly, and passionately worship Him in Spirit and in truth. Objectively, our best theology is dumb and our most complicated musical riffs are child's play. But God treasures every last bit of it because it comes from the hearts of His Spirit-anointed kids.

An experience overhearing my four-year-old little daughter taught me in one instant why this practice of singing is so valuable to God. Every night Karlee sings herself to sleep. The songs are extemporaneous, and if I'm being honest, they are fairly artless. She's not composing symphonies way beyond her years. She just sings about her friends in preschool and sings about her dollies and her tea set. One night while eavesdropping on her, through the door I heard her singing about how much she loves her daddy. The song went on and on about how her daddy is the best daddy and he likes to play quicksand monster and takes her to Starbucks.

Though she has told me she loves me a thousand times, listening to her sing it from her heart caused me to burst into tears. I was ruined right there in the hallway.

Paul told the Ephesians not to be drunk on wine but to live "under the influence" of the Spirit, singing songs, hymns, and spiritual songs. Vocalizing our love to God through song is mysterious and powerful. He loves it for the same reason rich guys love getting handwritten cards from their kids. He loves it for the same reason that I enjoy hearing spontaneous songs from my baby girl's heart. Those little choruses and hymns and spur-of-the-moment spiritual melodies—those expressions of your passion move God. And in return His Spirit moves on you, filling you to overflowing with His very self.

ALL Y'ALL

Paul's simple phrase "be filled with the Spirit" is packed with meaning that doesn't always punch through in the English text. In the Greek text this statement is plural, meaning that it applies to all of the believers in Ephesus, and by extension it applies to all believers. Being filled with the Spirit isn't for some elite super-saints who manage to attain "real spirituality." It's for every Christian. All of Jesus's disciples should be participating in the regular filling of the Spirit that is available to them. Growing up in the South, we had a way of referring to everyone. It is that delightful Southernism, "y'all." However, most northerners don't know that the plural of "y'all" is "all y'all." Paul is speaking to all y'all—every believer needs to be Spirit filled on an ongoing basis. Paul's context is primarily community filling and community submission to one another, first in the church and then in the family.[6]

ONGOING SUBSEQUENT EXPERIENCES

One of the most fruitless debates in the body of Christ today is whether the baptism of the Spirit happens simultaneously—at the time of conversion and regeneration—or whether it is a subsequent experience to salvation—that is, it happens as an extra-salvation event to empower the believer for service. Whatever camp you land in on that issue, we can all agree that we need to live continually filled with the Spirit through worship and spiritual disciplines.

If you believe that Spirit baptism occurs at the moment of your rebirth, then you need to enter a life of continual filling of the Spirit's presence. If you believe Spirit baptism is a subsequent experience to your conversion, then you also need *lots of subsequent experiences* through continual Spirit filling. Paul's emphasis in the Greek text is on the continuous nature of the experience.[7] "Spirit filled" should never be a mere historical description of some experience you had in 1983 at youth camp.

Being filled with God's Spirit is a promise Jesus made in the Gospels. What earthly father would give his kid a brick when he asks for bread? What earthly father would give his darlings a venomous snake when they ask for a grilled fish? If men who are evil at heart can give good gifts to their children, how much more willing is God to give you the Holy Spirit if you ask? If you want to be continually filled, you can be. If you have a desire for God's Spirit—nothing will keep you from it.

INITIATING OR CONJURING?

Some commentators make a big deal out of the fact that Paul's verb for "be filled" is in the passive voice, meaning that we cannot fill ourselves.[8] While this is true, Paul does instruct the Ephesians to initiate Spirit filling through active praise and worship.

We can't fill ourselves. But we can actively engage in the behavior that potentiates the filling, which will result in the Spirit's influence on our thoughts and actions. He doesn't turn you into a mindless automaton who does His bidding as a passive instrument. He fills you as you engage in Spirit behavior. This will result in His influence on your thoughts and desires.

I have often wondered why each worship encounter doesn't turn out exactly the same as the previous one. There are times when I sing, make melody in my heart, and join my fellow believers in extolling the virtues of the King. But the experience is flat and I don't sense God's presence. It just feels like we sang a few songs. At the end I get up and I go home.

Does this mean that God isn't there—inhabiting our worship? No. He's there. His glory is always present. But there are times when He sovereignly manifests His presence. I have no say over when and where He does this, just as Adam and Eve had no say over when and where God manifested Himself in the garden. Even in paradise God's presence was somewhat hidden at times. Otherwise Adam and Eve would never have sinned because they would have always been aware of God's immediate presence in their midst.

The partial hiddenness of God is a great mystery that we may never understand this side of eternity. But each time we are filled to overflowing with God's Spirit and His joy, we are reminded that a day is coming when we will step into the full beam of His glorious presence for eternity. Someday the kingdoms of this age will acknowledge Jesus as their rightful ruler. Then our vocation of spreading the knowledge of God to every corner and nook of this world will be brought to completion.

LIVE UNDER THE INFLUENCE

The result of all this singing and reveling in the presence of God is that the Spirit will produce godly longings in us. God wants us to live under the influence of the Spirit, but we do this as we experience Him in all His fullness. Contrary to popular opinion, being filled with the Spirit is not synonymous to being "controlled" by the Spirit, but it does result in the Spirit enabling us with self-control. In the next chapter we'll explore what it means to replace our carnal desires with the Spirit's desires.

14

PILOT FLAME

Embrace spiritual desires.

We are halfhearted creatures, fooling about with
drink and sex and ambition when infinite joy is
offered to us, like an ignorant child who wants
to go on making mud pies in a slum because he
cannot imagine what is meant by the offer of a
holiday at sea. We are far too easily pleased.[1]
—C. S. Lewis—
Weight of Glory

MY FRIENDS MITCH and Jacki asked my wife and me to
house-sit for them while they went out of town. While I was
there, I noticed a small blue flame in their fireplace. I had never
used gas heat before, and so I didn't know what a pilot flame was.
I figured they had accidentally left their fireplace on.

My wife watched in amusement as I spent the better part of
the next hour huffing and puffing and blowing on the pilot flame.
I finally got the flame out and then called the owners to let them
know there was nothing to fear, old Jeff was here. They responded,
"Dufus. You're not supposed to blow out the pilot flame. It's supposed to stay lit."

In the same way, there are times in our Christian life when
our passion for God is raging hot. There are times when we're
exhausted and wonder where God is and why He seems so silent

in our circumstances. In all the seasons of life, is it possible to stay lit? Is it possible to keep our flame of zeal for God's presence hot even though the fires of gifts and opportunities dim at times?

It is possible. And it all starts with the flame of spiritual desire.

DON'T WANDER OFF

We've established that believers must come into relationship with God through Spirit baptism, which is a fire of rebirth and purity. This fire of rebirth and purity allows us to come into fellowship with a holy God who is off-limits otherwise. We are then empowered to be His people and thus His witnesses. We continually live filled with the Spirit as we practice a lifestyle of impassioned praise and worship to God. In this chapter we'll take the next step. We need to dial up our desire for God, and more specifically, for *God's desires*. Paul put it this way:

> So I say, live by the Spirit, and you will not gratify the desires of the sinful nature. For the sinful nature desires what is contrary to the Spirit, and the Spirit what is contrary to the sinful nature. They are in conflict with each other, so that you do not do whatever you want. But if you are led by the Spirit, you are not under the law.... But the fruit of the Spirit is love, joy, peace, patience, kindness, goodness, faithfulness, gentleness and self-control. Against such things there is no law. Those who belong to Christ Jesus have crucified the sinful nature with its passions and desires. Since we live by the Spirit, let us keep in step with the Spirit. Let us not become conceited, provoking and envying each other.
>
> —GALATIANS 5:16–18, 22–26

Walking by the Spirit means to obey in faith. It is a trusting obedience to Christ's teaching and God's Word. It is to be attentive to the Spirit's promptings, conviction, and supernatural disclosure for your life. When we practice walking, or trusting

obedience, the Spirit will energize and activate our faith to produce godly desires, which creates godly character in us. Again,
this is not mechanical, but it is experiential. There is a "powerful
and experiential—supernatural, if you will—presuppositional
basis" for this life in the Spirit.[2]

When I was four years old, I lived in an apartment complex
with my mom, dad, and older brother. It had snowed the night
before, which rarely happened in Virginia, and my mother wanted
to take my brother and me out to enjoy the freshly fallen snow.
At first we walked closely beside her and made little snowballs
and looked at the snow on the leaves. Then, as a curious, ram-
bunctious boy, I wandered off. I soon had wandered away from
my mother and ended up behind the apartment complex where
we lived. Because of the fresh snow, I didn't recognize where I was.
Also, I had no idea which door was the door to my apartment.

So I started banging on every door, crying my eyes out. When
no one answered, I'd move on to the next door and bang away
on it, crying my eyes out. Finally a neighbor couple without kids
opened their back door and let me in. I said, "What are you
people doing in my house?"

They replied, "This is our home. You know, we recognize
you, and I bet your mommy is very worried." They invited me in,
made me some hot chocolate, and waited for someone to show up
to get me. Finally my mother found me, and she thanked them
for watching me.

Do you know what happens when you fail to walk in step with
the Spirit? You wander away. You get lost. And you may even try
a lot of doors before you make it back to Him.

Paul's message to the Galatian Christians was, "Don't wander
off, folks. Walk in step with the Spirit. He is your teacher, and He
is your leader. You need to pay attention to His voice, forsaking
the voices of the flesh." Walking in step with the Spirit produces
the desires of the Spirit and minimizes the desires of the flesh.
Keeping in step with God's Spirit through obedient faith will
produce passion for God in us, which has an anesthetizing effect

on carnal impulses. But in order to walk in the Spirit, you need some help because you have a powerful foe working against you.

There Is Much Conflict in You

The second thing Paul tells the Galatians is that they needed to know there is a powerful war going on within each of them. It's as if you have spiritual schizophrenia. You have this internal fracas raging in you all the time. "The flesh," Paul says, "desires the opposite of the Spirit. The Spirit desires what is contrary to the flesh." Let's unpack that.

Realize that you are your own worst enemy.

Paul's primary concern for the Galatians was not what the devil was doing in their midst, but rather it was the self-inflicted damage. The sin that lives in us is a powerful enemy to the Spirit's desire for us. This enemy never goes away, and no matter how well you suppress him, the first time you let down your guard, the old you will lead a prison riot and attempt to take over. He desires what is contrary to the Spirit (Gal. 5:17).

He'll lie through his teeth to you too. The old self will tell you he's rehabilitated. He'll swear that he's reformed and will never do it again. But don't trust him. The sinful you will wage war against your soul. This is why Paul told the Ephesians to "put off your old self" who was being corrupted through evil desires (Eph. 4:22). This is why Peter warned the exiled believers to "abstain from sinful desires, which wage war against your soul" (1 Pet. 2:11). Our primary combatant in this war on evil is our old, corrupt sinful nature. We live in the already-but-not-yet kingdom. Already we have God's power to live with the desires of the Spirit. Already we have resurrection power at our disposal to do the works of Jesus. But Jesus hasn't consummated His kingdom yet. We still fight the menacing gremlins of past desires and past failures. But that old self is already on notice. He's crucified with Christ, and you have been raised to life.

Realize that this enemy has been defeated.

Your sinful nature will never stop loitering around, waiting for an opportunity to reassert his control over you. If you let him, he'll do a leg takedown and put you in the sleeper hold—then it's lights-out! But you have the power of the Spirit to live in triumph over this sinful you.

This is why Paul urged the Galatians to be "led by the Spirit," which results in self-control—or rather, Spirit-enabled self-control. Paul stated to the Roman Christians, "What shall we say, then? Shall we go on sinning so that grace may increase? By no means! We died to sin; how can we live in it any longer?" (Rom. 6:1–2). Paul insisted that they live in new life (v. 4). Because they have been set free from enslavement to sin (vv. 6–8), they now have the ability in the Spirit to live obediently to the pattern of Christian teaching (vv. 15–18), resulting in a pure life before God (v. 19). This was all made possible through the Spirit (Rom. 8:1–11). You are under no obligation to live according to the sinful nature. Jesus stated, "If the Son sets you free, you will be free indeed" (John 8:36). The Spirit desires what is contrary to the flesh (Gal. 5:17). You have the resources of heaven to live as Jesus did. Your sinful nature is defeated and crucified on Jesus's cross.

Realize that this enemy has an ally.

On your best day as a disciple, you are still in danger of being deceived and tricked into sin.

Did you know that most people don't believe there is such a being as a personal devil?[3] That doesn't surprise me. If I were Satan, I'd make them think I didn't exist, either. But I assure you, he is real. And he is the most powerful ally the old you has in this battle between your desires. He is a treacherous collaborator who persistently supplies your flesh with the provisions necessary for the old you to make a comeback. Your flesh is like Satan's man on the inside, his double agent. Your old self is his link to making inroads into your life again. If you relax or take a vacation from Jesus, your old self will gain strength and lead a surge against you.

If you want to keep the pilot flame lit for Jesus, you have to keep your enemies weakened. Jesus has overcome the power of sin and darkness, and you have to start living in the Spirit's power.

This is why Paul told the Ephesians to not give the devil a foothold (Eph. 4:27). They were to take their stand against the enemy, the devil (Eph. 6:11), and show him the business end of the gospel (v. 17). Peter stated, "As obedient children, do not conform to the evil desires you had when you lived in ignorance" (1 Pet. 1:14). Your old self will be constantly supplied by this evil dissident called Satan, but your ally is the Spirit, and a powerful ally He is.

One of Us Does, One of Us Doesn't

But what happens when we starve the desires of our sin nature, are filled with God's Spirit, and live in obedient trust to God's Word? Something organic and mysterious takes place. Our lives become gardens of the Spirit, producing a harvest of righteousness. It's no accident that Paul used an agricultural metaphor to the rural Galatian Christians (Gal. 5:22). He told them not to wander off but to walk in step with the Spirit, to refrain from gratifying the desires of the flesh, and to instead produce the fruit of a life in the Spirit.[4]

When my wife and I first bought our house, it had a beautiful vegetable and fruit garden in the corner of the property.

Trouble is, I hate gardening.

I particularly disliked rhubarb, which was the main fruit plant growing in the garden. The novelty of the hard work of tending it soon wore off, and eventually it started to look like someone was not tending it. Long grass and weeds began to grow up between the plants. Stray animals in the neighborhood had poached some of the produce, and I didn't water the plants—ever!

So after a couple of years I went out to the garden and dug up all the plants, then I sprayed a chemical called "ground scorch" or something like that. I did everything short of setting it on fire. For years that garden didn't produce.

Then I noticed some trees growing up in the garden. After a few years my cottonwood trees grew there and began to multiply in the rich soil. Before I knew it, I had about a dozen trees in that spot. I liked the trees. The foliage provided cover from the wind, shade from the sun, and a visual barrier between my neighbor and me. Also, the trees didn't require any maintenance. But after a few years, some of the trees began to break and die and fall into my neighbors' yards.

So I had to get my chain saw out, and I trudged through the thick little forest in order to cut some of them down. I cleared out the old ones, trimmed the good ones, and cut the tall grass. That's when I saw something amazing.

The produce and rhubarb plants had grown back. I hadn't seen them in years, and there they were. I was amazed at the resilience of this fruit. I was astonished at the power of a planted seed and deep roots. It's the power to produce something even though neglected and ignored. After breathing a sigh of amazement, I quickly got my tools, cut them down again, and sprayed more ground scorch on the spot.

I just hate tending gardens.

Now, my neighbor's garden is a sight to behold. It is well manicured, watered, and maintained. Each year at just the right time he harvests a little micro crop of tomatoes, corn, and—you guessed it—rhubarb. One of us tends his garden, and the other doesn't. One of us harvests a crop, and the other has to go to the grocery store for corn and fruit. One of us has the satisfaction of a well-tended patch of land that produces good from the earth, while the other is too busy to care about all of that.

Paul's analogy for the Galatians isn't in the abstract. They were farmers. They understood how critical it was to cultivate the soil and produce a crop. This is just what the Spirit does in our lives. Some believers have the seed, they have the soil, but they have done some very damaging things to their heart. The ground can still produce, and once in a while they'll surprise you with a hail-Mary-end-zone good deed. But for the most part they're lazy Christians who just don't want to put the work into fighting the good fight. Then they justify their laziness under the guise of "keeping it real" or "being authentic and nonreligious," which is usually code for "spiritually lazy."

Other believers are like my neighbor. They work the soil; they till it and cultivate it. They come out and fix the broken and weed out the bad. They protect it with a barrier, and they tend it well. They also harvest a crop of the Spirit. Their lives produce the Spirit's fruit of righteous living:

- They have a selfless love for others.

- They show patience, enduring pain and hardship.

- They have genuine gladness of heart.

- It seems they're always at a cease-fire with those around them.

- They are merciful with broken people.

- They offer a kindhearted response to those who wrong them.

- They exhibit genuine goodness from the heart.

- They follow through on their commitments (Gal. 5:22–23).

These character qualities appear effortless from a life that is led by the Spirit of God. It's not because they get up every day and check these things off their religious to-do list. It's because they get up every day and they have espresso and Jesus. They have communed with the Spirit in prayer and contemplation. They have suppressed the desires of the flesh by walking in step with the Spirit and have replaced those sinful desires with spiritual desire. Walking in the Spirit begins with obedience and results in God's Spirit transferring His own desires to us.

Then, He plunges us into seasons of loss and suffering. The

refiner's fire must do the work of burnishing our character until it shimmers in the light of His glory. This is what makes us fit for seasons of abundance—it is a refined inner man who shines with the light of godly desires.

And sometimes we blow it and need God's grace and forgiveness. Sometimes we snap at our spouses or assume something we shouldn't, or we cut someone off in traffic. We're not perfect, and we're not "just forgiven" as the bumper sticker wrongly suggests. We are in progress—sowing to the Spirit, reaping a harvest of righteousness, growing and making headway in our spiritual formation. We live with the pilot flame of love for Jesus always lit, always prepared to flip the switch to raging hot.

We Want His Wants

When we walk in the Spirit, the Spirit starts the process of gradually replacing our corrupt desires with the desires of God. We want what God wants. We seek what He seeks. Jesus said that if we seek the kingdom rule of God and His path to righteousness, then all things will be added to us. C. S. Lewis called this the "first reward of our obedience."[5] Our first prize is a desire for more of God. It doesn't happen all at once. It happens like a tide slowly raising a grounded ship.[6]

Looking back over my life, I recognize that my past is littered with activities, sports, hobbies, and interests that I no longer care about that much. Every one of those hobbies I used to be passionate about. But the passion fades. My prayer is that God won't be one of my hobbies, but that He'll be the Lord of my very existence. I pray that my mystical union in the Spirit with Him will be a never-ending passion—a pilot flame of desire that the Spirit can turn raging hot at any moment of His choosing. But in order to keep this fire lit, I must walk in step with the Spirit, battle my internal selfishness, and produce the kingdom's fruit.

15

UP THE ANTE

Embrace spiritual disciplines.

> I had never *practiced*. Practiced until it
> became the second nature, the first skin.
> Practice is the hardest part of learning, and
> training is the essence of transformation.[1]
> —ANN VOSKAMP—
> *One Thousand Gifts*

LOWELL STREIKER WAS a fresh-faced pastor of an established church, and he was eager to do well at his new assignment. The church finances improved in his first year there, so they decided to launch a capital campaign to double their budget. Their plan was to canvass the community wearing T-shirts, asking members and non-active attenders to "up" their pledge.

"If only we had a slogan...some catchy motto or jingle around which to rally our campaign," he thought. Then it came to him. He knew just what the slogan needed to be.

The following Sunday Streiker placed boxes full of T-shirts at the front of the sanctuary. He pulled one out and eagerly displayed it to all the canvassers. It was in that moment as he proudly read their new slogan that he realized just how memorable of a campaign this was going to be. The front of the shirt read, "I Upped My Pledge..." But when he turned it around, on the back it read, "Up Yours!" Laughter from the congregation echoed through the sanctuary, and Pastor Streiker never quite regained control of that worship service.[2]

In the same way, if we want more of the Spirit's power unleashed in us, then we are going to have to up the ante on our commitment. If we want to keep our flame of zeal lit for Christ, we're going to have punch it up in the area of spiritual disciplines.

Jesus taught the disciples that "everyone who is fully trained will be like their teacher" (Luke 6:40). Likewise, Paul told the Corinthians, "Everyone who competes in the games goes into strict training" (1 Cor. 9:25). He also instructed the Ephesians to bring up their children in "the training and instruction of the Lord" (Eph. 6:4). He commanded Timothy to "train yourself to be godly" and taught him that the Scriptures were critical in that training (1 Tim. 4:7; 2 Tim. 3:16).

If we want the harvest of righteousness in our lives, it takes practice. Disciplined Christianity produces lean and fit believers who are prepared for service in Jesus's kingdom. In contrast, lazy Christianity produces flabby and powerless disciples who lack that competitive edge, are ignorant of the Scriptures, and are stuck in intellectual neutral. Without spiritual discipline we will remain tantrum-throwing little terrors who never quite become like Jesus the Master. In an earlier chapter we noted the interplay between the Spirit and God's Word. In this chapter we'll focus on two essential disciplines of spiritual life. We'll explore how specifically to master God's Word and how to hear the Spirit's voice through prayer.

It Means What It Meant

Have you ever posted something on Facebook only to have some "friends" totally misunderstand what you were saying? This happened to me recently, and it felt awful because the person failed to give me the benefit of the doubt. They brought their emotional "luggage" to my conversation. This is called *transference*.

Transference takes place when you unload or project your own issues onto someone else.

Truthfully, people do this to the authors of Scripture all the time. We come to the text with our own predilections and world-view baggage and then import *our* meaning to *their* words—meaning they never intended. The first task of the writer is to say what he means, and his second task is to keep people from supposing he means something other than what he means. We should seek to understand the authors of Scripture in their contexts and within the framework of their culture. The Bible means what it meant. With every line of Scripture we should ask, "What did this *mean* to say?" not "What can this be *made* to say?" This axiom is what sets us apart from the cults, which pour their own meaning into Scripture all day long.

God's written Word is the lexicon of the Spirit, meaning, God's written Word has the semantic range that the Spirit will often use to speak directly into our spirits. If the principle or promise in Scripture is roughly equivalent to your situation and the Holy Spirit is infusing those words, making them come alive to you in that moment—then you are listening to the Spirit's voice in the text. But taking a promise that has nothing to do with your situation and reading meaning into it is not the Spirit's work. That's just you. We need to know what the authors of Scripture originally intended to say in their historical situation because applying its intent is critical to our development.

So at the end of the day, our task is not merely a historical one.[3] It is an empathetic one. Our task is to identify with those original readers so that we may hear the Scripture's meaning, respond to the Spirit's promptings, and apply its intent. The Spirit will never say anything to you that contradicts what is already revealed in God's Word.

DON'T STARVE THE DOG

Not too long ago our family got a cute little black dog. The kids named him Oliver. Oliver is half Yorkshire terrier and half Shih Tzu. I bought the dog because my kids had been begging me for a dog for years. I finally relented, though I immediately laid down *the law*! I was not going to feed the dog, groom the dog, pick up after the dog, clean up his messes, housetrain him, walk him, or anything else. Oliver was *their* dog, not my dog.

A week after I brought him home, Kerri took the kids to her grandma's house in Montana and left the dog with me for the weekend. So much for "the law"!

So I decided to lighten up and bond with the animal. Fortunately my wife knew me well enough to know that she had to leave a detailed list of things to do for him, along with a schedule and yada yada yada. I wanted no part of it. But the puppy was irresistibly cute, so I decided to follow her instructions.

The minivan drove off, and I went up to the kitchen and got out the list. Boy, was it long. There were, like, six things to do on that list. I read it, then I reread it. I figured I had it down. The rest of that weekend I spent *applying* that list. Now, I'm sure you would agree that it would have done me no good to simply be able to read it and correctly interpret my wife's meaning. I needed to go beyond interpretation and fill the dog's bowl, take him out during the day, and give him a bath. Without a commitment to application, my wife would have returned to a very messy house and a starved dog.

That's true of Scripture also. The task is never done until we practice Jesus's teaching and address the issues of life. You may think you're getting "full" on Sunday because you've rightly heard and understood the Word. But until you apply it, you're spiritually starved.

It never ceases to amaze me that when God needs to correct or teach me, He'll do it through the little hypocrisy police who live in my house. My kids will catch inconsistency faster than anything. I am constantly on the lookout for the Spirit's living voice in the context of my life. I will often hear a message from God through my interactions with my family. That's where the tires hit the pavement for me. I need God to flip on the light switch, showing me opportunities to apply His Word. If you've put in the time to study and have done your homework, your next job is to listen for those Spirit-inspired moments in everyday stuff. The Spirit will instruct you in the context of life. We must "up" our commitment to apply the Word. This takes diligence and practice. But eventually if we keep at it, we will develop an automatic response of applying Scripture in our context.

SPIRITUAL MUSCLE MEMORY

When I first started playing guitar in my early twenties, it would take me forever to change from one chord formation to the next. My instructor would show me what a G chord looked like. Two minutes later I had my fingers in the right position and would strum a half-muted, ugly-sounding chord. But I kept at it. Eventually I progressed so that I became a guitar instructor myself, teaching others how to do it.

The secret was that I spent hours training my fingers where to go and developing what is called "muscle memory." As the body repeats the same pattern, neural pathways are carved out in the brain, and the motor task gets easier with repetition. What others see as effortless riffing is the accumulation of hours spent going slow, repeating patterns, and memorizing new finger placements.

The same is true in the Christian life. If you have a problem with coveting your neighbor's stuff, then you need to memorize Paul's command in Philippians chapter 4 on contentment. Every time you see their boat or Harley or something you really wish you had—place your spiritual fingers on the right strings and strum an ugly chord. The first few times you obey it will feel awkward and unnatural. But after about the thousandth time you'll have developed a pattern of godly response. The same is true with lust. If you find yourself lusting after every shapely female that crosses your path, then you need to memorize Jesus's saying about dealing drastically with sin. Then, when the situation presents itself—*strum* that passage, even if you badly paraphrase it. Then do it a thousand more times, and you'll begin to retrain your body to the pattern of Spirit living. This is the sort of thing Paul had in mind when he wrote to the Romans about obeying the pattern of Christian teaching:

> But thanks be to God that, though you used to be slaves
> to sin, you wholeheartedly obeyed the *form of teaching* to
> which you were entrusted. You have been set free from
> sin and have become slaves to righteousness.... But now,
> by dying to what once bound us, we have been released
> from the law so that we serve in the *new way of the Spirit*,
> and not in the old way of the written code.
> —Romans 6:17; 7:6, emphasis added

Paul stated that we serve in the new way of the Spirit. And this is far more than mere Scripture memorization. Memorizing the contents of Scripture is a good thing. But more importantly we need to train our bodies, bringing them into subjection to the Spirit through repeated and sustained obedience to the Word. We must memorize the pattern of life, which is the new way of the Spirit versus the old way of slavish and Spirit-less conformity to a religious code.

As we repeat the pattern in faith, the Spirit mysteriously energizes us and the Word becomes flesh again. The Spirit will meet you at the confluence of your trust in and obedience to God's Word. We learn His Word, interpret it rightly, and listen for the voice of God's Spirit to teach us in the context of life. This is what Paul referred to as "Spirit-taught words" (1 Cor. 2:13).

The first discipline we must master is applying the Scriptures to life. We must "up" our commitment to God's Word, applying it as the Spirit forms and shapes us into the image of Jesus. The second discipline we must engage is the habit of prayer, or holy conversation with God.

OPEN A CHANNEL

Several years back I went with a missions team to Guatemala. I didn't realize that we would be in communication silence for nearly two weeks—no Internet, no Facebook, no e-mail, and no cell phone capability. Not to mention, we were housebound for the first week due to the very dangerous neighborhood in which we were located.

For the first few days the team was euphoric, ebullient, and giddy. We spent the first week remodeling the church house where we were staying, and it was great. But after day four without any communication with home, we all started to get a little cranky. Then cabin fever started setting in. When the Internet was finally working in the home, we had a small window to send a single Facebook message to our families, and we got one brief phone call with loved ones. It was like a lifeline.

I found that it was increasingly difficult to focus on the mission at hand because I was so preoccupied with wanting to hear from my family. I felt starved for the voices of my wife and children. When I returned home and finally got off the plane, I just couldn't get enough of them.

I think many believers today are starving for the Spirit's voice. Prayer is the key because prayer is conversation. We need to open lines of communication with God through prayer. We have an inherent need to be heard and to hear the voices of our loved ones.

Let me highlight a few tips on what Paul referred to as "praying in the Spirit," that is, praying with the Spirit's help. This isn't exhaustive, but it will get you going in praying spiritual prayers.

Pray with one eye open

Paul taught us to be alert and to pray in the Spirit on all occasions (Eph. 5). "On all occasions" is about lifestyle, not emergency praying. For example, the healthier your exercise habits and lifestyle, the fewer trips you will make to the emergency room. In the same way, the healthier your prayer life, the less you need a Hail Mary prayer when the clock on your situation is running out. God doesn't just want to be there for you in a crunch; He also wants to be there for you in the calm. Lifestyle praying invites the Spirit to inhabit every scintilla of our existence. But this happens as we make prayer the automatic response of the redeemed heart. Paul tells the Ephesian believers to "be alert and always keep on praying for all the saints" (Eph. 6:18). Essentially he wanted them to transition from "on occasion" praying to "every occasion" praying. I call this praying with one eye open. They were to be alert to the needs of others and be ready to pray at a moment's notice. Lazy, occasional prayers at holidays and meals are a non-starter for God. The Spirit will work powerfully through an alert, well-exercised prayer life.

Pray big

Let me ask you. When is the last time you really went big in prayer? I know, I know. We don't want to be selfish and self-serving in our prayers. James warned us about God's provision drying up due to misspent resources. Wasting God's assets on frivolous nonsense and then asking Him to fill our coffers again is a sure recipe for silence from heaven (James 4:3). But notice in that same passage that James tells those believers to go big. He states, "You do not have, because you do not ask God" (v. 2). When we pray, we are addressing a God with unimaginable power. This God is also sovereign, which means He can do whatever He wants whenever He wants to do it. But we don't want to err on the side of blaming God's sovereignty for every non-answered prayer. This will lead to a tepid and anemic prayer life.

It's like my wife, who was always afraid to ask her father for anything growing up. To her, he just seemed inaccessible because of his size and his gruff beard. In reality, her dad is a kind and generous person. But his size and "griz" always kept her expectations in check. After we were married, she told me, "I had no idea how generous he was. I should have approached him and asked more often."

All too often we picture our heavenly Father as a crotchety old deity who is busy spinning worlds and regulating the physical laws in the universe. Surely this brooding old gent is too busy tinkering with physics to entertain our requests? Not true. As I've learned over the years, people of great means are always flattered by great "asks." They are honored that we consider them capable of the request. And God is honored when we aim high. It demonstrates that we have a high opinion of His capacities. So don't be afraid to pray big.

Pray small

This same God who formed galaxies and main sequence stars also made atoms and subatomic particles. God cares about the big stuff and the small stuff. He cares about your job and your family and the issues of your heart. He troubles Himself over your conversations and your relationships. He wants to be intimately involved in your daily life. Any theology that teaches that the Spirit *only responds* to big prayers has missed the point. God isn't just the author of the big stuff. He also made the small stuff.

What kind of father would I be if I pushed my children away every time they wanted to show me a macaroni-and-construction-paper school project? Do their school projects change the way I operate as a professor or a pastor or a supervisor? No. Do I need their projects to help me in the big things? Absolutely not. But as a good father I care about their little worlds. Not because I think turkey hand paintings are works of art. But because I adore the little person who made that turkey hand painting. My interest in the smallness of their worlds is because of the greatness of my love for them.

During my second church plant in my twenties I had developed a solid theology of God's sovereignty—or so I thought. I went through several years when I was convinced that God's sovereignty meant He had no time for my trifling concerns. I stopped asking God for miracles or messages. I stopped looking for Him, and you know what happened? I stopped finding Him. As a result, my passion for God began to wane. Long-distance relationships are always difficult to maintain. God isn't an absentee Father. He is ready and willing to be engaged in your world. If He knows how many hairs are on your head and He has the tally on every molecule in your body, then surely He cares about your job and your interests. Reach out to Him in prayer, and include Him in small matters. Life is mostly small stuff.

I used to picture God as the ultimate scientist—His knowledge of the universe must be mind-boggling. But I've discovered that God is just as interested in gardening and painting as He is in tinkering in His heavenly lab. He loves getting His hands down in the soil of our lives, working it and making something useful out of it. He loves the mess of the art studio—getting paint and clay all over His hands and clothes. Paul didn't say that we were God's lab experiments; he said we were God's works of art (Eph. 2:10). You're not a problem the Spirit has to solve; you're a work of art in progress, and Jesus cares about all the details of your life. So ask Him to redeem it and inhabit it. Pray big. And pray small.

Pray normal

I don't typically like to dissect and parse what is commonly called the "Lord's Prayer." I know a lot of people do that because they are looking for a prayer formula. But that's kind of missing the point. I think the broad strokes are the "meat" in that meal. In its historical context the Lord's Prayer is a lesson in contrasts. Jesus's prayer was infinitely shorter than the *tefillah*, the long and wordy prayer recited in the synagogues. Unlike the *tefillah*, His prayer had no curses for enemies but instead contained a clause on forgiveness for those who've sinned against us.

Jesus's prayer was also intimate compared to the formal prayers of the Pharisees. He called God "our Father in heaven." Jesus's language lacks the pretentious yattering of formal religion. His language is so normal. He just speaks to God as a father and doesn't dress it up with a bunch of religious gobbledygook. Jesus's prayer was expressed in normal human language, not the vapid religious jargon of the Pharisees. This is why we say that prayer is "conversation" because Jesus Himself used conversational, not formal, language to speak to God.

Similarly, most of Paul's prayers in his letters are normal too. He prays for the believers' safety, their knowledge growth, their enlightenment, and their progress in Christ. He prays they will be strengthened in their inner beings with God's Spirit and that the Spirit will work powerfully in their midst. Paul's prayers for the saints were normal, not paranormal. We should speak to God in our normal human language. We don't need to tidy it up or rehearse it. God wants it raw—straight out of your heart and expressed in conversational language. This too is spiritual praying. And we need to "up" our commitment to talk to God like He's an actual person.

Pray weird

That said, we shouldn't be afraid to allow the Spirit to help us when we just can't find the words. Some of you will pray in what I refer to as a heavenly speech form. This type of prayer is directed to God and not to men. It is unintelligible and in public worship requires translation (1 Cor. 14:2–3). Paul uses normal human language as an analogy of this kind of spiritual praying (vv. 9–12). And since a thing is not identical to that which it is analogous, he is obviously not talking about praying in normal human languages. He is referring to praying in a strange and unusual language inspired by the Spirit.

This can be a regular prayer language that bypasses the human intellect (vv. 13–19). If you have this gift, great. Paul stated he wished all the Corinthians had this gift, which shows that not all of them did have it. He also expressed his desire that they all be single like him. But not all of them had or should have had that gift either.

Now, if you don't have this ability to speak to God in spiritual languages, you should be open to the Spirit helping you pray in your weaknesses—when no language will do, human or otherwise. Paul refers to this in Romans as "groans that words cannot express" (Rom. 8:26). Paul's context in Romans 8 is the Spirit's comfort for believers in the face of suffering and the future hope of a redeemed world (vv. 18–21). The Spirit Himself intercedes and assists us to pray in those situations when words simply cannot express our grief and stress and desperation.[4] I've experienced this on occasion. Paul states that the world is rumbling and on the verge of new creation. The earth eagerly awaits the redemption of God's children—because everything hinges on our resurrection. If I'm reading Revelation correctly, the new heavens and new earth will follow our resurrection to an incorruptible state. It's as if this place is about to blow and a new world is about to be born.

As I mentioned before, I pastored a struggling church in a small town. I nearly worked myself to death trying to pastor that church. But my best efforts and best prayers weren't effective. After three years the church was near failure, and I was busy tying knots at the end of my rope, barely hanging on.

To make matters worse, one of my primary leaders had met with me for coffee and informed me that he and his family were leaving. I think I took it well in the coffee shop. But when I got into the car to drive away, I began to experience internal rumblings. It felt like that moment when you realize you're in an earthquake and there's nothing to hold on to because everything is moving. I drove away trying to ignore the seismic activity going on below.

But before I knew it, I had exited the freeway into a rest area, and when the car came to a stop, that's when I came unraveled. I experienced a deep, sorrowful travailing in prayer, and it came in waves. The Spirit shook me deep within, causing aftershocks of intense weeping and grief. It took about twenty minutes or so before the rumbling stopped. I had never been so desperate for God, and I had never encountered the Spirit quite like that. It was primal, unintelligible, and powerful! During this period as a church planter, I prayed at times with these same groanings from the Spirit—rolling and tumbling out of me came expressions of prayer that wouldn't be intelligible to the nearest angel, let alone a human being. But it was a travailing, or a spiritual anguish, from the deep well of my human spirit. I look back on that season in my life and think of how weird my prayers were, so unusual, but I wouldn't trade the intimacy that I developed with Jesus for anything!

I'm not saying this is the way you should pray every day. Most of the time your prayers should be normal. We should be open to praying with the Spirit and with our intellects fully engaged.

Are you facing the impossible—a foreclosure on your home, no prospects in a jobless economy?

Are your children far from God and haven't shown the slightest interest in Him?

Are you facing a devastating loss?

Then take it to God. Allow yourself the space to pray these "wordless groanings" as the Spirit helps you through it. Paul says that the Spirit is your intercessor. So don't be afraid to pray weird when you need to.

Marks of the Amateur

Don't be in a hurry. Living in the supernatural power of spiritual disciplines takes time. Quality matters. And God isn't in a hurry. Author Mark Buchanan puts it this way:

> "Being in a hurry. Getting to the next thing without fully entering the thing in front of me. I cannot think of a single advantage I've ever gained from being in a hurry. But a thousand broken and missed things, tens of thousands, lie in the wake of all the rushing."
>
> Through all that haste I thought I was making up time. It turns out I was throwing it away....The heart is the place the busy life exacts its steepest toll.[5]

You can't rush devotion. But you can run yourself ragged trying to check everything off your list. You can whip yourself into a walking maelstrom of activity as you rush from one thing to the next. We have to develop the skills associated with spiritual passion. That takes time. We need to give ourselves the real estate to develop and grow, and the space to transform.

When you get married, you're oversupplied in feelings of devotion and love. When you get divorced, you realize that you had not learned the skills—mastered the habits—of passion. You'd just been running on the vapors of a low tank—spent by the seasons of life.

Jesus learned and practiced these habits of passion for God. The Gospel writers show this on many occasions, and Luke just comes right out and says it: "He [Jesus] went to the Mount of Olives, *as He was accustomed*" (Luke 4:16, NKJV, emphasis added). It was Jesus's custom, or regular habit, to get alone with God. Diligence of habit is the mark of the proficient. Lazy believism and marginless living are the marks of the amateur. We need to follow Jesus up that well-beaten path to the top of our Mount of Olives. We need to make this our regular custom.

This is why we need godly mentors who can model these habits for us. My friend and pastor Kurt has shown me how to do this. No matter the situation at Eastpoint Church—no matter how hairy the scenario—I've watched Kurt go up his Mount of Olives. Whatever personal trial or challenge comes into his life, the loss of loved ones, a devastating diagnosis, I have watched Kurt go up the mountain to meet with God—to cultivate, renew, replenish, and reinvigorate his passion for God.

Researchers have discovered that it takes ten thousand hours to master something. If you want to become a master of piano, cello, sports, chess, or writing—it takes about ten thousand hours of sustained, persistent practice. This is how long it takes the brain to attain a mastery of anything.[6] Researchers were shocked to discover that it doesn't take a "natural" or a genius to become world class. It just takes practice. In the same way, if you and I want to become proficient and competent in the Spirit, we will have to put in the time. We'll have to up the ante on spiritual disciplines. This may cause you to have to get up a bit earlier or cut out a favorite TV program—but the dividends of a life spent in the disciplines of passion will pay off.

16

ACT YOUR "AGE"

Embrace spiritual growth.

And if we by faith venture into the wild and
as-yet-undiscovered places of God, the gift of
holiness will become our gift of wholeness, too.
By His touch, we can trade our sorrows for
His joy, our ashes for the oil of gladness.[1]
—MARK BUCHANAN—
The Holy Wild

TODDLERS ARE THE most uninhibited creatures on earth.
They just exist in the now. Toddlers haven't lived long
enough to become cynical, to care about their weight, or to stress
over unpaid bills. These miniature people just live to play—with
our car keys and all the stuff in our wallets. And they are end-
lessly amused at things that our world-weary eyes don't even see
anymore.

This is why my wife and I love to dig out old videos of our
kids. We laugh and even tear up as we watch them investigate the
world with voracious wonder. We miss their chubby cheeks and
their hooked-on-phonics attempts at language. We bust a gut as
they sample old cereal on the kitchen floor and conflate "I'm a
Little Teapot" with "The Hokey Pokey."

But often in our reverie we are reminded how difficult that
stage was too.

"I got to go potty, Daddy"—I pause the video. Then we snap

back to reality. We remember all the diaper changes, potty training "mis-fires," the tantrums and their discovery of "Mine!" and "No!" Then we thank God for their progress. God has built in certain payoffs for parents as we successfully transition them into the next stage of their growth. I miss their fat baby faces, but I don't miss stinky pants and bedtime meltdowns.

One of our primary responsibilities as parents is to help our kids transition into becoming real, live grown-ups. Our role is to give them the spiritual and social tools they'll need to navigate the choppy waters of adulthood.

BOOMERANG CHRISTIANS

It's tragic to watch a young adult fail to successfully transition into maturity. This is known as "failure to launch," which results in the "boomerang effect"—adult children who don't succeed at becoming adults and so they ricochet from one job to the next until they land back at home (assuming they moved out in the first place). No demographic is more adversely affected by this than young men.

In his insightful book *Boys Adrift*, Dr. Leonard Sax identifies five factors that have contributed to the cultural epidemic of unmotivated young men: 1) an overly feminized educational system that disengages boys, 2) excessive use of video games, resulting in increased aggression and a lack of real-world engagement, 3) overdiagnosing and overmedicating boys, resulting in diminished drive, 4) a toxic diet that literally emasculates boys—resulting in lower sperm counts and a drop in bone density, and 5) the abandonment of traditional religious structures that intentionally graduate boys into manhood.[2] The net result of this cultural shift, according to Dr. Sax, is that boys experience stunted growth and a diminished drive. Growing young men who ought to have advanced into manhood still act like boys—immature and living in their parents' basement playing video games well into their thirties and forties.

As tragic as this is, we must recognize that this can also happen in a spiritual sense. The church today is full of "boomerang Christians." These believers have been in the church a long time. But as my pastor Kurt often says, "They grew *old* but didn't grow *up*." Unless we are intentional in our growth, we will exhibit immaturity and a lack of holiness. We will fail to act our "age." We will forever languish as spiritual toddlers, bumping around and making messes in the Christian life. Spiritual growth takes place as we learn to act according to the value system that characterizes the coming age—the kingdom of God.

Jesus taught that the coming age wasn't going to put an end to this present age—not just yet. Instead, the kingdom would be established right over top of this old order with resurrection power. N. T. Wright states, "We could cope—the world could cope—with a Jesus who ultimately remains a wonderful idea inside his disciples' minds and hearts. The world cannot cope with a Jesus who comes out of the tomb, who inaugurates God's new creation right in the middle of the old one."[3] The new creation has already been initiated right over the top of the old order of things. And the Spirit is the key to this. The Messiah, as the bearer of the Spirit, would inaugurate this new age by sending His people the Spirit of God to live within them.

So we have the ongoing clash of two ages—this one and the coming age of the kingdom. This is an age characterized by evil and emptiness.

INVISIBLE JIM

My kids love collecting action figures. We recently came across an old toy that seemed irresistible. The toy is called "Invisible Jim." The manufacturer behind Invisible Jim says it encourages children to use their imaginations. The toy comes with a colorful package and lots of cool slogans on the box. Jim has a "lack of darting eyes" and "realistic fake hair." The box only cost the US manufacturer pennies to make but sold for around nine dollars.

There's only one problem. Jim isn't in the box. In fact, there's nothing in the packaging. It turns out that Invisible Jim is just a gag gift. The colorful, attractive box is empty.

That's the way sin is. You buy the packaging, but there's nothing inside. It's a cheap thrill that leaves you empty. This is what characterizes "this age." Here's how the apostle Peter put it: "For you know that it was not with perishable things such as silver or gold that you were redeemed from the empty way of life handed down to you from your forefathers" (1 Pet. 1:18). Peter wrote that we've inherited an empty package. This age is characterized by the vacuous and unsatisfying pursuits of the sinful nature: the lust of the eyes, the pride of position, and the wanton pursuit of self. But something deep within us knows that there's more to life than this.

This age is humming with activity—people doggedly pursuing all of the wrong sources of life and mastering the wrong skill sets. They're chasing a life that will forever evade them until they come to faith in Jesus and are remade by the Spirit.

Masters of Awesomeness

My brother and I used to have a fascination with Kung Fu Theater. Every Friday night, WRLH channel 35 would play Kung Fu movies from 9:00 p.m. to midnight. We'd get in our sleeping bags and watch the Kung Fu masters go at it. During every commercial break we'd jump up and...

Kung Fu say what? Hayee-Yah!

...practice our moves on each other.

Our favorite moments in the movies were the training scenes. The formula goes like this: You take a person with heart who is a diamond in the rough. He meets an old master at the craft who then puts the young fighter through a grueling training process designed to maximize his potential. When they finally get another chance to fight the big boss battle, this young prodigy is now ready to throw down.

So my brother and I decided to devise our own Kung Fu training process. We found some rusty old darts in the attic and threw the darts at each other while blindfolded. We figured if we could learn to block the darts while blindfolded without getting pinned to the wall or needing a hepatitis B shot, then we were on our way to becoming Kung Fu masters.

Then we decided to test our reflexes. So we unscrewed the tips from our practice arrows, then shot the blunted missiles at each other from a short distance with Daddy's fiberglass bow—trying to catch the arrows. Afterward we took Daddy's old pile of bricks behind the shed and practiced breaking them with our bare hands. Then we got the phenomenal idea to practice "brick dodging," where we drew a circle at both ends of the dirt basketball court. Each circle had a pile of bricks beside it. The combatants were allowed to stand in the circle and could duck and dodge the bricks being hurled in their direction. But the trainees could not step outside the circle. This only resulted in one trip to the ER.

And what training would be complete without mastering weaponry? We sawed off Mom's broom and mop handles, wrapped them in black electrical tape, and attached a chain to each end of the sticks. Voilà! Instant nunchucks. We'd practice hooking each other's legs with nunchucks while running.

Mastering these important elements meant that we were on our way to becoming legends of awesomeness. Mastering our fear. Mastering our control of pain. Mastering our reflexes.

Of course, all of these forms of "training" were dangerous and dumb and should never have been tried. We later discovered that we spent all of our time mastering the wrong things. We hadn't become masters of Kung Fu; we were just mastering Kentucky Fu. We had replaced the power and elegance of Tae-Kwon-Do for the weakness and clumsiness of "Redne-Kwon-Do!" These pursuits were empty and fruitless and just plain wrong.

Busy? Yes.

Masters? No!

FILLING THE EMPTY BOX

Before we were transformed by God's Spirit, we were awfully busy trying to extract life from others. In fact, the sinful nature has become an expert at extorting life from just about everything around it. We need life. And we're good at trying to squeeze it out of others. It's just that we have spent our lives mastering the wrong skills.

The drug user, the shopaholic, the food addict, the sports junkie, the sex fiend—they're all just trying to fill the empty box. It is a most holy place, that box. It's an inner sanctum that only the Spirit was meant to occupy. Yet we trash this sacred ground—the sanctuary of our hearts—with the sacrilegious and the silly. Some activities are in and of themselves harmless, and some are dreadfully toxic. But all pursuits of life apart from the author of life essentially have the same effect—we are still left empty.

No buzz that comes from this age will ever fill you. Because this age, as Peter stated, is empty. It is void of the Spirit's life. God's presence is the real substance meant to fill our vacant souls. This is why Jesus sent the Spirit. Paul stated that Jesus "gave himself for our sins to rescue us from the present evil age, according to the will of our God and Father" (Gal. 1:4). Jesus came to inaugurate God's kingdom rule, bringing us the new life of the Spirit. The presence of the Spirit means that the two ages coexist. And we are supposed to act according to the kingdom age, not this one.

Paul told Titus, "The grace of God that brings salvation has appeared to all men. It teaches us to say 'No' to ungodliness and worldly passions, and to live self-controlled, upright and godly lives in this present age" (Titus 2:11–12). God's grace isn't available just so we can get our tickets punched and escape hell. Notice Paul says that His grace teaches us to live godly lives in this present age of darkness, this epoch of turmoil, bedlam, rage, and injustice.

How do we live holy? Well, He isn't called the "Holy" Spirit for nothing. The Spirit comes to begin a work of purity in us. He shows us the way.

RADIOACTIVE SOIL

Paul told the Philippians, "Whatever is true, whatever is noble, whatever is right, whatever is pure, whatever is lovely, whatever is admirable—if anything is excellent or praiseworthy—think about such things" (Phil. 4:8). The reason it is so critical that we devote ourselves to a pure thought life is because our thoughts will drive our direction. The thoughts are the fertile ground of our actions.

During the Japanese earthquakes and nuclear meltdowns of 2012, a high level of Cesium contaminated the soil for miles around. Japan was paralyzed for months due to contaminated soil. You can't grow edible crops in radioactive soil. A pure thought life starts with keeping out foreign elements that will contaminate the ground of your heart. Let's get specific. The Holy Spirit doesn't want you watching pornography. That stuff is like mental heroin. It's radioactive. And bad soil cannot produce a pure crop for the kingdom.

When I started losing weight, I went to the gym and lifted weights and ran on the treadmill every day. But I wasn't losing much. Then a friend said something to me that was both a revelation and a shocker. We were sitting over a meal, and he was eating a plate full of vegetables and lean chicken and I had a plate full of junk food. He said, "There's your problem right there. You're putting garbage in your body. *All the working out in the world won't do you any good. Diet is everything.*" I was eating too many empty and toxic calories.

The same is true in our spiritual lives. Spiritual diet is everything. You cannot experience significant change of direction if you're still living off the slurry and the slop of this failed age. Pure living starts with a pure heart, pure devotion to spiritual activity, and a pure thought life.

Nothing Plus Nothing Gives You Nothing

Before a newborn baby has any knowledge of food or understands the nature of sustenance, he knows what it means to be hungry. Instinctively our hungry stomachs tell us that such a thing as food must exist—before we can even comprehend the nature of the thing that we crave. Likewise, I do not know that God exists because I have seen Him. I know that such a thing must exist because the deep, yawning emptiness in my spirit hungers for His life.

The trouble is, a starving man will eat just about anything. And our starving world has tried to extinguish the pangs of spiritual hunger with pleasure, sex, and all sorts of stuff. But these things have left men hollow. They are like the boy who was promised a feast and arrived to a party decorated with streamers and balloons and supplied with all the cake he could eat. Once the sugar buzz wears off, his little belly growls for something real—something of substance. We ache for the Spirit to fill us, and we spend our lives pursuing flimsy knockoffs made to look like the real thing. But they are not. And ultimately they cannot really fool the God-hungry heart.

People who fill up the empty box with more emptiness will only reap emptiness. Nothing plus nothing gives you nothing. But those who sow pure thoughts will reap a harvest of pure living. It starts with a pure devotion but ends in the alignment of the rest of our person. Philosopher Dallas Willard put it so well: "The heart cannot be renovated if the other aspects of the person remain in the grip of evil."[4] We harvest what we plant. If we scatter to the flesh, we will reap destruction. If we sow to the Spirit, we will reap a harvest of righteousness.

Kingdom Swag

This world is scrambling for life. They may be unaware that they thirst for 100-proof God, yet they have imbibed and subsisted on the watery swill of this failed age. And while they fill up on it, we Christians are told that we are all a bunch of old-fashioned relics from a bigoted and bygone era. We need to get out and "live a little." We should open our minds and not be so narrow and intolerant. We should get some new swag.

Puh-leese! Do you want to know the truth?

They don't have a plan. They're just aching souls trying to find real life. But that life only comes through the Spirit of God, and it isn't available in the values or practices of this fallen world. The alternative to following these lemmings (who ironically imagine themselves to be rogues and trailblazers) is to follow Jesus and allow Him to invade your life with His transforming presence and power. This is the really progressive, fringe idea in our day. It is to live in the flame, refusing to settle for a domesticated, housebroken Christianity. We need the "tonic of wildness."[5] The remedy for tame and Spirit-less religion is risky faith—embracing this mysterious and beautiful person called the Holy Spirit.

You're one limitation away from a breakthrough, one shattered barrier away from a miracle. Ironically, your only limitation to deep communion with the Spirit is the one you impose on yourself. What limits have you put on your experience with the Spirit? Where is the line you won't venture past? No one ever discovered the limits of anything by cautiously sneaking up to it. Don't be afraid. Cement your feet in the foundation of sound doctrine and go blundering and caroming into the unknown. Embrace the work of the Spirit.

Tune out the voices of the madmen of this age who only offer hackneyed and shopworn solutions to real life. And pay equally little attention to the self-appointed guardians of Christendom who tell you that the fullness of the Spirit is not for you today.

Bless their hearts, they are wrong.

A life of pure devotion and kingdom living awaits you. And it means that you will have to embrace the awesome and unwieldy mystery of God's Spirit, and it means that you will have to stop scarfing up the pabulum of this age. You will need to grow up in your salvation. You will need to stop telling others how "real" and "relevant" you are, and you will need to live in the light of the Spirit's conviction.

Living in God's transforming presence entails being empowered to meet your obligations—to love God passionately and to serve others selflessly. It will require you to discover and deploy extra grace—Spirit gifts and abilities. God wants to anoint you for kingdom living. As you ratchet up your disciplines, as you replace your sinful passions with the desires of the Spirit, then and only then will you experience the God who wants to invade your life with His transforming presence.

EPILOGUE

I HOPE YOU WERE not looking for the last word on this subject, as you have no doubt discovered that I have not written it. Instead I have attempted to write a book with wonder, imagination, exegesis, and the occasional surprising insight. My prayer is that you reengage this ignored and marginalized person of the Trinity—the Spirit. My hope is that you seek His presence and long for God to fill you from the heart outward. And I hope your patience will indulge me one last story (or two).

Not long after I told a friend of mine that I no longer believed in "the prophetic" work of the Spirit, God saw fit to blow up my tidy, reductionist theology.

I was the new associate pastor on staff at a large church and was charged with overseeing the small group and discipleship ministries in the church. I had scheduled a training meeting with all my group leaders and had prepared a full day of lessons, group interactions, and the occasional break for refreshments.

I usually script out my notes and follow them pretty closely. At one point in the training I mysteriously felt compelled to go off my notes and give an analogy about the importance of character and commitment. I said, "And I don't care if you've been married for twelve years. If he spends all of his time out in the shop working on his 1969 Camaro and she spends all her time in the garden and working in the house—you're off track. You need to serve Jesus together, not as two single people..."

Suddenly an older couple in the group of leaders burst into

tears, right in the middle of the meeting. It was apparent that I needed to adjourn and find out what was going on. I dismissed everyone and met with them for a few minutes. Through teary eyes they told me that the Spirit had just spoken to both of them. It turns out that was the day of their twelfth anniversary, and on the way to the training they had the biggest argument of their married lives. It was over him spending too much time in his shop with his '69 Camaro and her spending too much time in the garden and the house. The Spirit had their number. And we all three sat there in awe that God's Spirit cared enough to speak to them and that He would use me to do it.

Paul stated that prophecy is encouragement. The essence of all of the Spirit's activities is healing, comfort, encouragement, confrontation, and correction. We shouldn't be afraid of God using us to speak into the lives of our friends and neighbors. God wants to give us supernatural insight that we may help build His kingdom on earth.

Don't be afraid of the mystery. Embrace it. Own it. And let the Spirit work mightily through you.

A Spirit of Love, Power, and a Sound Mind

Your greatest barrier to the fullness of life in the Spirit is fear and sin. But the Holy Spirit is not a Spirit who engenders fear or inspires terror. He is a Spirit who advocates, comforts, and empowers. Yes, we are apprehensive about Him at first. But there is nothing to fear here. You're in good hands. You're in God's hands.

I remember the first time I ever shot Daddy's shotgun. I was four years old. Now, I wasn't by myself. My dad took out his double-barreled twelve-gauge shotgun and put it in my little hands. He knelt behind me and held the big shotgun. I was firmly in his arms, totally enveloped by his strong and powerful frame. Even so, I pulled the trigger, and the gun knocked me on the ground. I started bawling. My dad picked me up and said,

"There. You see. You're still alive. It will only kill you if you're on the other end of it!"

From that moment on, I was never afraid to shoot a shotgun. I knew they were powerful. I knew they could be unmanageable and dangerous in the hands of a novice. But I also knew that they could be incredibly useful and powerful tools in the hands of one who has been instructed, who has been trained in gun safety.

Don't be afraid of the Spirit. Don't be afraid of His gifts or His manifestations in your life, or what supernatural thing He might do in you. Don't fear or recoil from the transformation process. Jesus was sent to save you from the devil's hell. The Spirit was sent to save you from a life of paralyzing doubt, selfish living, and crippling anxiety.

> For God did not give us a spirit of timidity, but a spirit of power, of love and of self-discipline.
> —2 TIMOTHY 1:7

NOTES

1—The Other One

1. Craig S. Keener, *Gift and Giver* (Grand Rapids, MI: Baker Academic, 2001), 18.

2. Barna.org, "Most American Christians Do Not Believe That Satan or the Holy Spirit Exist," April 10, 2009, https://www.barna.org/barna-update/article/12-faithspirituality/260-most-american-christians-do-not-believe-that-satan-or-the-holy-spirit-exis#.UjiJVnTD8dU (accessed September 17, 2013). Barna notes that an additional 9 percent disagreed "somewhat" that the Spirit was only a symbol of the Christian faith. This leaves only a solid 25 percent who firmly believe in the Spirit as a person.

3. Barna.org, "How Different Generations View and Engage With Charismatic and Pentecostal Christianity," March 29, 2010, https://www.barna.org/barna-update/faith-spirituality/360-how-different-generations-view-and-engage-with-charismatic-and-pentecostal-christianity#.UjiJ1XTD8dU (accessed September 17, 2013). Barna noted that most believers labeled themselves "charismatic" yet resisted the notion that the Spirit does miraculous things in our day-to-day lives.

4. Gordon Fee, *Paul, the Spirit, and the People of God* (Peabody, MA: Hendrickson Publishers Inc., 1996), xiv.

5. Gordon Fee, *God's Empowering Presence: The Holy Spirit in the Letters of Paul* (Peabody, MA: Hendrickson Publishers Inc., 1994), 1.

6. A. W. Tozer, *Mystery of the Holy Spirit*, reprint (Alachua, FL: Bridge-Logos, 2007), 39.

7. William Barclay, *The Gospel of Matthew* (Louisville, KY: Westminster John Knox Press, 2001), 15.

8. Fee, *God's Empowering Presence*, 32.

9. Ibid., 29–30.

10. Ibid., 28.

2—There's No App for That

1. Ted Olson, "U2's Bono Says He'd 'Like to Be' a Christian," *Christianity Today*, February 1, 2001, http://www.christianitytoday.com/ct/2001/februaryweb-only/43.0b.html (accessed September 25, 2013).

2. Jeffrey Spier, *Picturing the Bible: The Earliest Christian Art* (New Haven, CT: Yale University Press, 2008), 51–52.

3. Larry Hurtado, *Earliest Christian Artifacts: Manuscripts and Christian Origins* (Grand Rapids, MI: Eerdmans, 2006), 60–70.

4. Alister McGrath, *Christianity: An Introduction* (Oxford, UK: Blackwell Publishing, 2006), 331.

5. Michael J. Anthony, *Exploring the History and Philosophy of Christian Education: Principles for the 21st Century* (Grand Rapids, MI: Kregel, 2003), 194–195.

6. Daniel Burke, "How Many Bibles Do We Really Need?" Christianity.com, http://www.christianity.com/Christian%20 Foundations/The%20Bible/11639814/ (accessed September 25, 2013).

7. George Barna, "Six Megathemes Emerge from Barna Group Research in 2010," Barna.org, December 13, 2010, https://www .barna.org/culture-articles/462-six-megathemes-emerge-from -2010?q=biblical+literacy (accessed September 25, 2013).

8. Luis Lugo, "U.S. Religious Knowledge Survey," The Pew Research Forum, September 28, 2010, http://www.pewforum .org/2010/09/28/u-s-religious-knowledge-survey-preface/ (accessed September 23, 2013).

9. Shemuel Safrai, *Compendia Rerum Iudaicarum ad Novum Testamentum: Section One, The Jewish People in the First Century*, vol. 2 (Minneapolis, MN: Fortress Press, 1976), 948. It should be noted that the *bet sefer* schools were not formally set up until the appointment of Joshua ben Gamala in the AD 60s. However, since the Jamnian rabbis were in a position to idealize their education in far grander terms, we should accept that some elementary education was readily available to both Jesus and His countrymen. After all, neither Joshua ben Gamala nor the later rabbis created the system *ex nihilo*— they simply proliferated an existing educational system.

10. Jacob Neusner, *From Politics to Piety: The Emergence of Pharisaic Judaism* (New York: KTAV Publishing House, Inc., 1979), 64, 67. Though most secular biblical scholars downplay or criticize the New Testament's picture of the Pharisees as pure parody, Neusner shows that even in the Rabbinic literature there were very negative portraits of the Pharisees. It is likely that the New Testament authors are describing a particular kind of perushim due to their overly zealous use of Oral Torah. It is also likely that these perushim morphed into the post-Jamnian rabbinic schools.

11. James Jeffers, *The Greco-Roman World of the New Testament* (Downers Grove, IL: IVP Academic, 1999), 253–257. It should be noted that because of their penchant for sacred texts, Jewish and Christian followers were typically more advanced in literacy education

than their pagan peers. It should also be noted that Josephus brags about Jewish students to his pagan rival, Apion (*Against Apion* 2.18).

12. William Law, *The Power of the Spirit* (Fort Washington, PA: CLC, 2012), 19.

13. Daniel B. Wallace, "Who's Afraid of the Holy Spirit? The Uneasy Conscience of a Non-Charismatic Evangelical," in Daniel B. Wallace and M. James Sawyer, eds., *Who's Afraid of the Holy Spirit?* (Dallas: Biblical Studies Press, 2005), 8. Wallace is a former charismatic and a professed cessationist. He prefers to call himself a "pneumatic" Christian and is a scholar who believes in the power and activity of the Holy Spirit for today—just not in regard to what he refers to as the "sign gifts." However, this is curious because the phrase "sign gifts" is entirely absent from Paul's own writings.

14. Ibid., 9.

15. Barbara Aland and Kurt Aland, *The Greek New Testament*, 4th rev. ed. (Stuttgart: United Bible Societies, 1994), 493.

16. Kenneth Bailey, *Jesus Through Middle Eastern Eyes* (Downers Grove, IL: IVP Academic, 2008), 96–97.

17. Woodrow Kroll, *Taking Back the Good Book* (Wheaton, IL: Crossway Books, 2007).

18. Jack Deere, *Surprised by the Voice of God: How God Speaks Today Through Prophecies, Dreams, and Visions* (Grand Rapids, MI: Zondervan, 1996), 27–28.

3—Another One

1. Catholic Online, "St. Cyril of Jerusalem on the Living Water of the Holy Spirit," May 14, 2013, http://catholic.org/homily/yearoffaith/story.php?id=50917 (accessed September 25, 2013).

2. Gordon D. Fee, *The First Epistle to the Corinthians*, NICNT (Grand Rapids, MI: Eerdmans, 1987), 4.

3. Craig Keener, *1–2 Corinthians*, NCBC (New York: Cambridge University Press, 2005), 3.

4. David Gill, *1–2 Corinthians, Zondervan Illustrated Bible Backgrounds Commentary* (Grand Rapids, MI: Zondervan, 2007), 102–106.

5. James D. G. Dunn, *Jesus and the Spirit: A Study of the Religious and Charismatic Experience of Jesus and the First Christians as Reflected in the New Testament* (Grand Rapids, MI: Eerdmans, 1975), 304–307.

6. Oscar Broneer, "Hero-Cults in the Corinthian Agora," *Hesperia* 11 (1942), 128–161.

7. J. P. Moreland, *The Kingdom Triangle: Recover the Christian Mind, Renovate the Soul, and Restore the Spirit's Power* (Grand Rapids, MI: Zondervan, 2007), 168.

8. Ibid., 175.

9. D. A. Carson, *The Gospel According to John*, PNTC (Grand Rapids, MI: Eerdmans, 1991), 500.

10. Walter Bauer, *A Greek-English Lexicon of the New Testament*, rev. by Fredrick W. Danker, 2nd ed. (Chicago: University of Chicago Press, 1979), 618.

11. Carson, *The Gospel of John*, 500.

4—Treasure in a Chipboard Case

1. Stormie Omartian, *Lead Me, Holy Spirit* (Eugene, OR: Harvest House Publishers, 2012), 34.

2. Rich Winter, *Still Bored in a Culture of Entertainment: Rediscovering Passion and Wonder* (Downers Grove, IL: IVP Academic, 2002), 32–44.

3. LiveScience Staff, "Why We Get Bored," NBCNews.com, September 27, 2012, http://www.nbcnews.com/id/49192477/ns/technology_and_science-science/#.UNfENI7XETM (accessed September 25, 2013).

4. Aaron Smith, "Americans and Their Cell Phones: Key Findings," Pew Internet, August 15, 2011, http://pewinternet.org/Reports/2011/Cell-Phones/Key-Findings.aspx (accessed September 25, 2013).

5. Isaac Asimov, as quoted in Rosemary Jarski, ed., *Words From the Wise* (New York: Skyhorse Publishing, 2007), 18.

6. Winter, *Still Bored in a Culture of Entertainment*, 8.

7. William Lane Craig, *Reasonable Faith: Christian Truth and Apologetics* (Wheaton, IL: Crossway, 2008), 43, 50.

8. G. K. Chesterton, *The Essential Gilbert K. Chesterton* (Radford, VA: Wilder Publications LLC), 168.

5—Can You Hear the Sirens?

1. Donald Miller, *Blue Like Jazz* (Nashville: Thomas Nelson Inc., 2012), 53.

2. m. Qidd 4.14. This rabbinic passage states, "A man should always teach his son a cleanly craft, and let him pray to him to whom riches and possessions belong, for there is no craft wherein there is not both poverty and wealth; for poverty comes not from a man's craft, nor riches from a man's craft, but all is according to his merit." Many

Jews believed that there was a direct correspondence between one's faithfulness to the law and material blessing.

3. Bailey, *Jesus Through Middle Eastern Eyes*, 347. Bailey notes that loud and proud prayer is common in the Mideast as an outward show of righteousness before God. So Jesus's character is easily credible even by today's standards of pious praying.

6—The New and Improved You

1. Dallas Willard, *Renovation of the Heart* (Colorado Springs, CO: NavPress, 2002), 14.

2. Steve Jobs, "'You've Got to Find What You Love,' Jobs Says," Stanford commencement address, June 12, 2005, http://news .stanford.edu/news/2005/june15/jobs-061505.html (accessed September 25, 2013).

3. Alex Kuczynski, *Beauty Junkies: Inside Our $15 Billion Obsession With Cosmetic Surgery* (New York: Doubleday, 2006), 1.

4. ABC News, "Crime Blotter: Old Woman Leads Car Chase," December 2, 2004, http://abcnews.go.com/US/CrimeBlotter/ story?id=317890&page=1#.UNflGI7XETN (accessed September 25, 2013).

5. Steven M. Baugh, *2 Timothy*, ZIBBC (Grand Rapids, MI: Zondervan, 2002), 489.

6. As quoted by Bruce Lockerbie, *The Timeless Moment* (Westchester, IL: Cornerstone Books, 1980), 49.

7—When I Say "Jump!"

1. N. T. Wright, *Simply Christian* (New York: HarperCollins Publishers, 2006), 122–123.

2. Anne Lamott, *Bird by Bird* (New York: Random House, 1994), 21.

3. Gordon Fee, *Listening to the Spirit in the Text* (Grand Rapids, MI: Eerdmans, 2000), 140.

4. John Nolland, *The Gospel of Matthew: A Commentary on the Greek Text* (Grand Rapids, MI: Eerdmans, 2005), 234.

5. N. T. Wright, *Philippians* (Downers Grove, IL: InterVarsity Press, 2009), 45.

8—Unlimited Bandwidth

1. R. C. Sproul, *The Mystery of the Holy Spirit* (Carol Stream, IL: Tyndale House Publishers, 1994), 121.

2. *Justin Martyr to Athenogoras*, Ante-Nicene Christian Library (Edinburgh: T &T Clark, 1871), 64–65.

3. Dallas Willard, *Hearing God: Developing a Conversational Relationship With God* (Downers Grove, IL: InterVarsity Press, 2012), 142.

4. Alvin Plantinga, *Where the Conflict Really Lies: Science, Religion, and Naturalism* (New York: Oxford University Press, 2011), 318.

5. Philip Sigal, *The Halakah of Jesus of Nazareth According to the Gospel of Matthew* (Atlanta: Society of Biblical Literature, 2007), 92–93.

6. Nathan Drazin, *History of Jewish Education From 515 BCE to 220 CE (During the Periods of the Second Commonwealth and the Tannaim)* (n.p.: Mottelay Press, 2008), 5–38.

7. Jacob Neusner, *A Rabbi Talks With Jesus* (New York: Doubleday, 1993), 46–47.

8. Craig Keener, *The IVP Bible Background Commentary* (Downers Grove, IL: InterVarsity Press, 1993), 66.

9. See 2 Timothy 3:15.

10. Charles Gates, *Ancient Cities: The Archeology of Urban Life in the Ancient Near East and Egypt, Greece, and Rome* (New York: Routledge, 2003), 105–106.

11. Ibid. Particularly striking is the temple of Hatshepsut with an outer court leading to a secondary court and a terrace leading to a third court and finally an inner sanctum. The temple is surrounded by a portico, and with the exception of some features that are specific to ancient Egyptian religion, it appears to be laid out in similar fashion to the Jewish temple. Yet this temple predates the Jewish temple and for that matter the Exodus.

12. Dan Wallace, *Revisiting the Corruption of the New Testament: Manuscript, Patristic, and Apocryphal Evidence* (Grand Rapids, MI: Kregel, 2011), 27–29. This is a very fine critique of Metzger and Ehrman's standard text *The Text of the New Testament: Its Transmission, Corruption, and Restoration.*

13. N. T. Wright, *Surprised by Hope: Rethinking Heaven, the Resurrection, and the Mission of the Church* (New York: HarperCollins Publishers, 2008), 293.

9—The Extra-Natural Power of God

1. Mark Batterson, *Primal* (Colorado Springs, CO: Multnomah Books, 2009), 63.

2. Guillermo Gonzalez and Jay W. Richards, *The Privileged Planet: How Our Place in the Cosmos Is Designed for Discovery* (Washington: Regnery Publishing, 2004), 66.

3. Ibid., 183.

4. Ibid., 128–129.

5. Ibid., 57.

6. Ibid., 183.

7. C. S. Lewis, *Mere Christianity* (New York: HarperCollins Publishers, 2009), 38–39.

8. John Walton, *The Lost World of Genesis One: Ancient Cosmology and the Origins Debate* (Downers Grove, IL: InterVarsity Press, 2009), 16–17.

9. Wayne Grudem, *Bible Doctrine: Essential Teachings of the Christian Faith* (Grand Rapids, MI: Zondervan, 1999), 126.

10. Austin Hill and Scott Rae, *The Virtues of Capitalism: A Moral Case for Free Markets* (Chicago: Northfield Publishing, 2010), 25–28, 35.

11. Mishneh Torah, Shabbos 8:15, 21:18–31. Since the use of medicinal aids involved "crushing" or mixing remedies, this was thought to be forbidden on the Sabbath by the Pharisees. Jesus's challenge to this extreme law was that the law was intended for the person, not to be slavishly followed by the person.

10—Red-Shirt Christians

1. Justin Martyr, *Justin Martyr's Dialogue With Trypho the Jew*, vol. 1, trans. Henry Brown (Oxford: 1745), 166. Viewed at Google Books.

2. Walton, *The Lost World of Genesis One*, 72.

3. Wright, *Simply Christian*, 129.

11—Spirit-Gifted Love Machines

1. 1 Corinthians 13:8.

2. C. S. Lewis, *The Four Loves* (New York: Houghton Mifflin Harcourt, 1991), 3.

3. Mike Bickle, *After God's Own Heart: The Key to Knowing and Living God's Passionate Love for You* (Lake Mary, FL: Charisma House, 2004), 108.

4. Scot Mcknight, *The Jesus Creed: Loving God, Loving Others* (Brewster, MA: Paraclete Press, 2004), 6–7.

Part 3—Embrace the Mystery

1. Brennan Manning, *Ruthless Trust: The Ragamuffin's Path to God* (New York: HarperCollins Publishers, 2000), 107.

12—Built to Hold Fire

1. Tom Wright, "The Holy Spirit in the Church," Fulcrum Conference, Islington, April 29, 2005, http://www.fulcrum-anglican.org.uk/events/2005/inthechurch.cfm (accessed September 27, 2013).

2. Polymer Science Learning Center, "Some Uses of Fire," http://www.pslc.ws/fire/benefits/benefit2.htm (accessed September 27, 2013).

3. Mark Andrew Brighton, *The Sicarri in Josephus' Judean War: Rhetorical Analysis and Historical Observations* (Atlanta: SBL, 2009), 2–4.

4. Craig Keener, *The Gospel of Matthew: A Socio-Rhetorical Commentary* (Grand Rapids, MI: Eerdmans, 2009), 121.

5. Ibid.

6. James D. G. Dunn, *Baptism in the Holy Spirit* (London, UK: SCM Press, 1970, 2010), 32.

7. Ibid., 42.

8. Geza Vermes, *Jesus the Jew: A Historian's Reading of the Gospels* (Minneapolis, MN: Fortress Press, 1981), 52–57, 99. Vermes mentions the general disdain that all Jewish parties had for the rabble in Galilee. In fact, in all of the rabbinic literature, only two rabbis of note were from Galilean descent. The rest of them were considered uncouth ruffians who were beneath the Southern Jews—the Pharisees and Sadducees.

9. Dunn, *Baptism in the Holy Spirit*.

10. Wright, "The Holy Spirit in the Church."

11. F. F. Bruce, *Acts in NICNT* (Grand Rapids, MI: Eerdmans, 1988), 50.

12. John Levison, *Filled With the Spirit* (Grand Rapids, MI: Eerdmans, 2009), 15.

13. Ibid., 24.

14. Ben Witherington, *The Acts of the Apostles: A Socio-Rhetorical Commentary* (Grand Rapids, MI: Eerdmans, 1998), 132.

15. Victor P. Hamilton, *Handbook on the Pentateuch* (Grand Rapids, MI: Baker Academic, 1982), 80–81.

16. C. C. F. Keil and F. Delitzsch, *The Pentateuch in Commentary on the Old Testament* (Grand Rapids, MI: Eerdmans, 1975), 174.

17. Hamilton, *Handbook on the Pentateuch*, 82.

13—Under the Influence

1. John Baillie, *St. Augustine: A Biographical Memoir* (New York: Robert Carter and Brothers, 1859), 221. Viewed at Google Books.

2. It must be noted that there are essentially three different uses of the term "fullness" in the New Testament. There are sovereign "fillings" that do not appear to be precipitated by any activity of the recipient. Luke also tends to use "full of the Spirit" as a designation of quality or a description of the overall character of a person's life. However, in each of these cases it is doubtful that those who are characterized by the Spirit's work did not actually experience the Spirit's work. Again, we come back to the phenomenological experience of the Spirit as the primary referent.

3. Authors such as John Stott, Francis Chafer, John Walvoord, and recently John MacArthur have argued well for the "filling as control" theory. In each of these cases, however, the actual experience of the Spirit as an immediate phenomenon is overlooked and ignored and in a few cases even denied. Stott comes the closest to acknowledging that there is an actual experience of the Spirit's presence taking place in the heart or spirit of the believer. Though this is the dominant understanding of "filling" in evangelical literature, this view seems to have very little conceptual basis in the ancient world and has even less biblical evidence.

4. Fritz Rienecker and Cleon Rogers, *Linguistic Key to the Greek New Testament* (Grand Rapids, MI: Zondervan, 1976), 538.

5. Fee, *God's Empowering Presence*, 722–723. Fee makes it clear that Paul's use of "drunk" and "Spirit filled" are not comparative experiences but contrasting ones. That is, we are not "drunk on the Spirit" per se, but are filled with Him and are enveloped into the fullness of God so that we exhibit the fruit of the light and instruct one another. "Drunk" then, is a contrasting analogue—a juxtaposition as it were.

6. Ibid.

7. Rienecker and Rogers, *Linguistic Key to the Greek New Testament*, 538.

8. Fee, *God's Empowering Presence*, 721. Fee points out that Paul's use of *plerousthe en pneumati* in the Greek is of a varied nature. Sometimes he uses the accusative (Col. 1:9), sometimes descriptively as a genitive (Rom. 15:14), and also as a dative of means (Gal. 5:14). The Spirit is both the substance and the means by which believers are filled. And often in these passages the believer's activity potentiates or initiates the filling.

14—Pilot Flame

1. C. S. Lewis, *Weight of Glory*, as quoted in C. S. Lewis, *C. S. Lewis: Readings for Meditation and Reflection*, Walter Hooper, ed. (New York: HarperCollins Publishers, 1996), 35.

2. Fee, *God's Empowering Presence*, 433.

3. Barna.org, "Most American Christians Do Not Believe That Satan or the Holy Spirit Exist."

4. Fee, *God's Empowering Presence*, 444. Fee cautions against reading too much into the passive nature of "fruit" as the product of the Christian life. After all, Paul has already told them to actively engage the life of the Spirit, and most of the "fruit" passages of Paul are accompanied by imperatives in the Greek text. But our obedience only positions us to produce a harvest of the Spirit—which is the result of a changed nature.

5. C. S. Lewis, *Weight of Glory* (New York, HarperCollins Publishers, 1980 rev.), 28.

6. Ibid.

15—Do You Want More?

1. Ann Voskamp, *One Thousand Gifts* (Grand Rapids, MI: Zondervan, 2011), 56.

2. Lowell Streiker, *Nelson's Big Book of Laughter: Thousands of Smiles From A to Z* (Nashville: Thomas Nelson, 2000), x.

3. Fee, *Listening to the Spirit in the Text*, 11.

4. Fee, *God's Empowering Presence*, 574–575.

5. Mark Buchanan, *The Rest of God* (Nashville: Thomas Nelson, 2006), 45.

6. Malcolm Gladwell, *Outliers: The Story of Success* (New York: Hachette Book Group, 2008), 35–46.

16—Act Your "Age"

1. Mark Buchanan, *The Holy Wild* (Colorado Springs, CO: Multnomah Books, 2003), 151.

2. Leonard Sax, *Boys Adrift: The Five Factors Driving the Epidemic of Unmotivated Boys and Underachieving Young Men* (New York: Basic Books, 2007), 11–12.

3. Wright, *Surprised by Hope*, 68.

4. Willard, *Renovation of the Heart*, postlude.

5. Henry David Thoreau, *Walden & On the Duty of Civil Disobedience* (Rockville, MD: Arc Press, 2007), 189.

For more, you can connect with the author at his personal website: **JeffKennedy.tv**

JEFF**KENNEDY**.tv

Home   The Blog   About   The Book   Resources   Contact

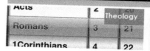

Don't Know Much About Theology?

Theology is nothing more than the study of God. And it isn't only for geniuses who work in academia. God wants all of us to be good students of his Word and Himself. In this section I'll share my thoughts on all things theological.

Are You Confident in Sharing Your Faith?

Believers typically cite 2 major reasons for not sharing their faith with outsiders: fear of rejection, and fear that they will not be prepared to answer objections. In this section, I'll share some helpful tips on how to share your story fearlessly.

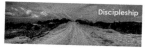

Are You a Disciple of Jesus?

Most believers aren't sure how to answer that question. They know they are saved, born again, maybe even filled with the Spirit. But they think of "discipleship" as only for the super-saints. In this section, I'll share my thoughts on debunking the myths and demystifying discipleship.

Ever Thought of Writing?

As a dad, a husband, and a teacher and writer, I have to manage a very busy life. I'll share many of the insights I've learned about growing in my faith, growing in my career, and my experience as a first time published author. Look for a free e-book on how to get started in your writing career.

I'm a lovesick disciple of Jesus, a husband to a lovely wife and the father of 4 hilarious little kids. I serve as the Executive Pastor of Adult Ministries and Discipleship at Eastpoint Church. I also teach as an adjunct faculty member for both Liberty University in Lynchburg, VA, and Moody's College of Distance Learning.

Praying for Daylight: Sheree   Edit Entry

Posted on October 17, 2013 by Jeff Kennedy • 12 Comments

Share   **f** Like 387   8+1 0   Tweet 4   Pin it   in Share

I watched as my father screamed his pain into the sky, from his bones, from his depths. I could see him rocking my sister in his arms. I knew it was her, but after the accident, I could hardly recognize her. I could hear my dad pleading with God to give her back. He and Mamma begged God not to take her. If sorrow had power she would wake up.

Stay Connected

email address

Subscribe

f   ✦   me   **v**   📷

Latest   Comments

PASSIO

PASSIONATE. AUTHENTIC. MISSIONAL.

Passio brings you books, e-books, and other media from innovative voices on topics from missional living **to a deeper relationship with God.**

Visit the Passio website for additional products and
TO SIGN UP FOR OUR FREE NEWSLETTER

PASSIO
THE ART OF AUTHENTIC FAITH

WWW.PASSIOFAITH.COM
www.twitter.com/passiofaith | www.facebook.com/passiofaith

12333